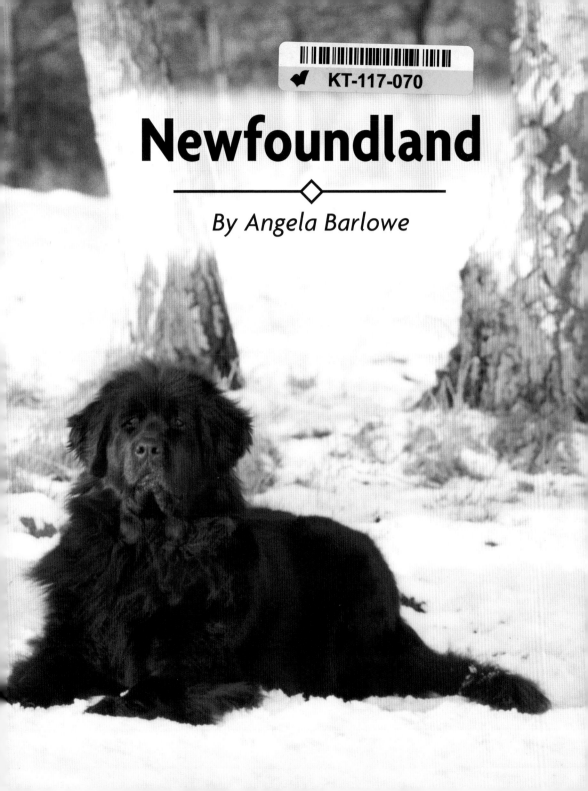

Newfoundland

◇

By Angela Barlowe

Contents

9 **History of the** Newfoundland

Dive into the Newfoundland's history and discover the various theories that surface about this gentle giant's beginnings. From Tibetan giants to European mastiffs to Bear Dogs and Vikings, the Newfoundland has proved a vital part of the lives of fishermen and seafarers for centuries, as a valued worker, rescue dog and all-around companion.

21 **Characteristics of the** Newfoundland

Find out if you're suited to be the caretaker of this giant, furry lover! While the Newf's sweet disposition and gentle ways recommend him as a wonderful home companion, this wonder dog also sheds and drools, requires buckets of food and the same amount of care and attention. Are you a Newfie person?

26 **Breed Standard for the** Newfoundland

Learn the requirements of a well-bred Newfoundland by studying the description of the breed as set forth in the American Kennel Club's breed standard. Both show dogs and pets must possess key characteristics as outlined in the breed standard.

32 **Your Puppy** Newfoundland

Be advised about choosing a reputable breeder and selecting a healthy, typical puppy. Understand the responsibilities of ownership, including home preparation, acclimatization, the vet and prevention of common puppy problems.

62 **Everyday Care of Your** Newfoundland

Enter into a sensible discussion of dietary and feeding considerations, exercise, grooming, traveling and identification of your dog. This chapter discusses Newfoundland care for all stages of development.

Physical Characteristics of the Newfoundland
(excerpted from the American Kennel Club breed standard)

Back: Strong, broad, and muscular and is level from just behind the withers to the croup.

Croup: Broad and slopes slightly.

Tail: Broad at the base and strong. It has no kinks, and the distal bone reaches to the hock.

Hindquarters: The rear assembly is powerful, muscular, and heavily boned. Viewed from the side, the thighs are broad and fairly long. Stifles and hocks are well bent. Hocks are well let down.

Coat: The outer coat is coarse, moderately long, and full, either straight or with a wave. The undercoat is soft and dense.

Flank: Deep.

Size: Average height for adult dogs is 28 inches, for adult bitches, 26 inches. Approximate weight of adult dogs ranges from 130 to 150 pounds, adult bitches from 100 to 120 pounds.

Color: Recognized Newfoundland colors are black, brown, gray, and white and black.

Training Your Newfoundland   **84**

By Charlotte Schwartz
Be informed about the importance of training your Newfoundland from the basics of housebreaking and understanding the development of a young dog to executing obedience commands (sit, stay, down, etc.).

Health Care of Your Newfoundland   **119**

Discover how to select a proper veterinarian and care for your dog at all stages of life. Topics include vaccination scheduling, skin problems, dealing with external and internal parasites and common medical and behavioral conditions.

Your Senior Newfoundland   **151**

Recognize the signs of an aging dog, both behavioral and medical; implement a senior-care program with your veterinarian and become comfortable with making the final decisions and arrangements for your senior Newfoundland.

Index 156

Photographs by:
Norvia Behling, T. J. Calhoun, Carolina Biological Supply, Doskocil, Isabelle Français, James Hayden-Yoav, James R. Hayden, RBP, Bill Jonas, Dwight R. Kuhn, Dr. Dennis Kunkel, Mikki Pet Products, Phototake, Jean Claude Revy, Alice Roche, Dr. Andrew Spielman, Michael Trafford and Alice van Kempen.

Illustrations by Patricia Peters.

KENNEL CLUB BOOKS® NEWFOUNDLAND
ISBN 13: 978-1-59378-283-2

Copyright © 2004, **2009** • Kennel Club Books® • A DIVISION OF BOWTIE, INC.
40 Broad Street, Freehold, NJ 07728 USA
Cover Design Patented: US 6,435,559 B2 • Printed in South Korea

10 9 8 7 6 5

The gentle giant is a renowned water rescuer, blessed with a buoyant personality and swimming ability.

HISTORY OF THE

NEWFOUNDLAND

The Newfoundland is frequently called the "gentle giant" among dogs. He is a large and imposing dog whose massive size belies his sweet and noble temperament. The kindly Newfoundland is a sweet and devoted family companion. He is a faithful friend who will protect children and, indeed, his entire human family, as well as risk his life to rescue a stranger from disaster. Blessed with a willing and hard-working nature, the versatile Newfoundland will make every effort to please his owner at whatever task presents itself.

The origin of the Newfoundland has always been the subject of much speculation. One theory suggests that the Newfoundland evolved from the Tibetan Mastiff, an ancient breed that accompanied Asian warriors on their journey across the Asian continent, eventually entering North America at Newfoundland.

A second theory suggests a cross-breeding between Mastiffs, Pyrenean Sheepdogs and Portuguese Water Dogs sometime during the 15th and 16th centuries. In fact, these and other breeds are believed to have been used and cross-bred by the native Beothuk Indians to aid them with their fishing chores.

Another widely accepted theory holds that the breed descended from what were known as Bear Dogs, large working dogs that were brought over to the North American continent by Leif Ericsson and the Vikings in 1000 AD. Other accounts claim that when the Vikings visited Newfoundland during the second century, they witnessed the native fishermen working side-by-side with large black retrieving dogs. Further speculation suggests that those dogs were eventually interbred and cross-bred with the native wolves.

Whatever the true beginnings, the actual history of the Newfoundland will forever remain a matter of conjecture, adding to the mystique and majesty that surrounds this unique breed of dog.

HONORABLE MENTION
A plaque erected in Swansea, South Wales, honors a Newfoundland named Swansea Jack, who saved 27 people from drowning at Swansea in 1937.

The great Irish Ch. Milk Boy, who did so much to bring the breed to the attention of the Irish and English. Circa 1932.

with great lung capacity and powerful swimming ability, enabling him to fight strong ocean currents and swim long distances. His ship chores included hauling the fishing nets from the boat and then back once they were full. Easily large enough to rescue a drowning man, he frequently rescued people who had fallen into the sea.

The early seagoing dogs were transported in pens in galleys called the "dog walk." Their principal function aboard ship was to swim ashore with a boat line to aid in docking if a choppy sea prevented the ship from mooring at a designated shore. In similar fashion, during a disaster, the Newf also carried lifelines out to sinking ships to help save the victims from death at sea. Reports of Newfoundlands who rescued drowning victims or small boats are legendary in ancient naval history.

Tales of Newfoundland heroism also can be found in history books. A Newfie accompanied Napoleon Bonaparte on board his ship on his return to France from Elba. When Napoleon fell over-

The first documented record of a breed resembling the Newfoundland can be found in records of that country dating back to the 1600s, when dogs of their description were traded by North American residents. The dog served primarily as a ship dog in Newfoundland, rendering a wide variety of services to his seagoing human caretakers.

Fishing was the primary industry in Newfoundland at that time, and every fishing boat carried at least one Newfoundland dog as an important member of the crew. The Newf was blessed

LIFEGUARD DOG
The Newfoundland was sometimes called the Lifeguard Dog because of his many legendary life-saving feats in which he saved people from drowning.

board into the dark waters and could not be located by his crew, the Newf dove off the deck to rescue the waterlogged emperor.

A Newfoundland was aboard the ill-fated *Titanic* when it sank. Another Newfoundland was awarded the Meritorious Service medal by Lloyds of London for rescuing an entire shipful of people in 1919. It comes as no surprise that a Newfoundland was chosen to accompany Lewis and Clark on their famous river expedition to the Pacific northwestern coast of North America in 1803.

The Newfoundland's role as helpmate did not end when his fishing boat tied up at dockside. The dog was hitched up to a cart, the day's catch loaded, and he hauled the fish to town. Newfs also pulled milk delivery wagons and hauled firewood, leaves and other supplies, which often weighed up to 450 pounds, for great distances. Their docile nature and strong work ethic were great assets to the residents of these towns as well as to the seafaring community.

It is thought that as many as 2000 Newfoundlands were owned and actively working in the town of St. Johns in Newfoundland by the early 1800s. Their jobs included hauling cut firewood from the forests, pulling in the fishing nets and hauling cartloads of fish from the docks. The dogs worked singly and in teams of

three to five dogs, and were so conditioned to their specified routes that they could deliver their wares without human aid or intervention and then return to their homes to receive rewards of their favorite food—dried fish.

Newfoundlands were also pressed into service as postmen, delivering the mail between railway stations and to a chain of outpost settlements. Over frozen terrain, through dense forests and under harsh conditions too difficult for equine travel, hardy Newfoundlands labored in teams of up to seven dogs to deliver His Majesty's mail. In honor of their distinguished service to their country, the King of Newfoundland commissioned a postage

Daventry Coastguard was a Canadian dog that took high honors. When only ten months old, he had just two more points to win to become a full champion. Circa 1934.

exceeded only by his expertise in the water. In England, during the 1800s, every lifeguard station along the British coast was required to employ the service of two Newfoundland dogs to aid in rescue attempts. The Newf is well constructed for life-saving heroics in the water. His double coat has a soft, fleecy undercoat and a stiff, oily outer coat that repels water, allowing him to swim for hours and yet remain dry at his skin. His massive build and great strength and endurance are well suited to swimming in cold, rough water. He has webbed feet and, unlike other water-loving breeds, he swims with a breast stroke instead of a dog paddle. His loose, droopy flews add buoyancy and allow him to breathe while carrying something or someone as he swims.

The breed's natural water instincts also help him evaluate and handle a rescue according to

In Germany in the 1920s, the Newfoundland was of a much heavier type than the Newfs seen elsewhere. This dog was a German champion. stamp emblazoned with the head of the Newfoundland.

Those same characteristics that made Newfs superior working dogs also lent to their neglect and abuse as working animals. It is believed that many Newfies suffered needlessly, with some even dying from exhaustion. During the 1800s, a law was passed in Britain forbidding their use in commercial hauling ventures.

The Newfoundland's hard-working ability on land was

Eng. Ch. Brave Michael was bred by Mr. E. Heden Copus in 1929. He received his Kennel Club championship in 1933.

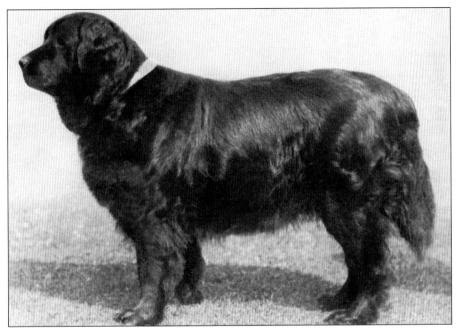

Eng. Ch. Mermaid became a champion in 1932. From a famous line of Newfoundlands in the UK, she was bred by Mr. G. Bland in 1928.

the needs of the victim. When a swimmer is conscious, the Newf will circle him and allow the swimmer to hold onto any part of his body while towing him to shore. If the swimmer is not conscious, the Newf will grasp the swimmer's upper arm in his mouth and tow him to safety. That upper arm hold causes the unconscious swimmer to roll onto his back with his head out of the water. If two Newfies are working as a team, each will instinctively take a different arm.

The Newfoundland's expertise as a water-rescue dog was recognized in numerous Victorian-era paintings during the 1800s. One painting by Sir Edwin Landseer, entitled "Saved," depicts a large black-and-white Newfoundland on a beach with a small boy who had just been rescued from drowning. A paint-

WAR RATIONS

During World War II, when food was scarce and often rationed, and many breeders were disposing of their breeding animals, a dedicated Newfoundland breeder, Mr. Handley, traveled countless miles across the countryside on his bicycle to collect leftover meat to feed to his dogs. He bred Newfs under the Fairfax prefix and produced many champions from his table-fed breeding stock.

Famous English portraitist, Sir Edwin Landseer, painted many black-and-white Newfoundlands. It was the artist's fondness for this color variety that led to its becoming known as the Landseer variety.

This painting by Sir Edwin Landseer of a black-and-white Newfoundland was exhibited in the National Gallery of British Art.

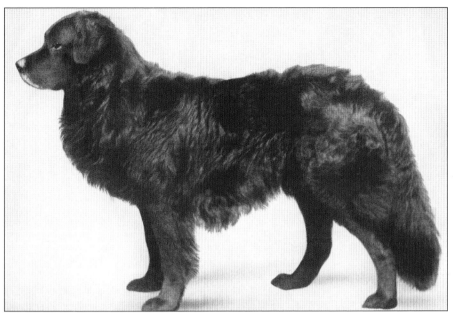

In 1899, Sir William MacCormack, President of the Royal College of Surgeons, owned the Newfoundland shown here. Due to the dog's heroics, friendliness and outstanding type, he became as famous as his master.

ing of the same scene by Currier and Ives is titled "He is Saved." Because the black-and-white Newfoundland was also featured in many later works by Landseer, this variety came to be known as the Landseer variety.

The breed was formally named in 1775 when George Cartwright named his own dog after the breed's native island. Five years later, the breed faced near-extinction when the government adopted a policy of one Newfoundland per household in an unsuccessful attempt to promote sheep-raising. The sheep population failed to increase, and the native population of Newfoundlands was decimated.

The new law forced many owners and breeders to ship their dogs out of the country, and many others were unfortunately destroyed. A few tenacious breeders, loyal to their precious Newfs, chose to ignore the decree and their clandestine efforts salvaged the breed in its native country.

The Newfoundland breed has been credited with, in the early 1800s, assisting in the beginnings of two of the retriever breeds: the ever-popular Labrador and the lesser known but equally talented Chesapeake Bay. The Labrador Retriever originated from a Newfoundland "type" of a smaller stature and with a shorter coat than today's Newfoundland.

Also, two Newfoundland dogs were rescued off Maryland's coast when the English ship on which they were traveling wrecked; these two became the foundation for the Chesapeake Bay Retriever.

During the mid-1800s, the Newfoundland played another important role in canine history, playing a major part in the survival of the St. Bernard. Around 1860, an epidemic of distemper almost eradicated the entire population of St. Bernards at the monastery in Switzerland. Because the two breeds are so similar in appearance as well as

function, with both breeds' being rescue animals that possess natural life-saving instincts, the monks imported several Newfoundlands to cross-breed and regenerate their stock. Some of these crosses inadvertently produced the first long-haired St. Bernards, a characteristic that is not compatible with the St.

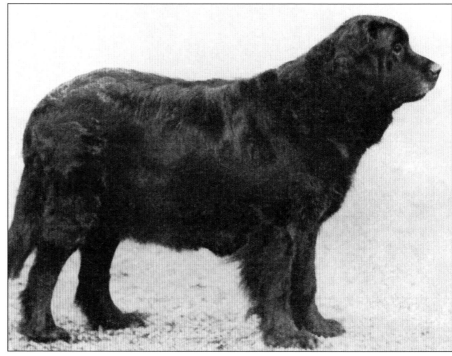

Eng. Ch. Netherwood Queen was bred by Mrs. F. McCann in 1926. She became a champion in 1930.

Bernard's primary duties of snow rescue. The longer hair collects ice balls, which add undesirable weight to the dog during a rescue attempt. Today, the St. Bernard occurs in both smooth and rough coats, the latter a credit to the Newf crosses.

Pre-World-War-I, the Newfoundland really thrived in England, which had become its adopted homeland of sorts. Top-quality dogs of British breeding were exported to the US and Canada, where they became the foundations of many renowned North American pedigrees. Unfortunately, the effects of the war were devastating in England, where breeding programs had to be discontinued. In addition to the war's disastrous effects, the stock of one major kennel was completely wiped out by poisoning.

In the late 1880s, a strong group of breeders was establishing itself in the US. The "father" of the modern breed came to the US directly from the breed's homeland, the isle of Newfoundland. Hon. Harold Macpherson, L.L.D, had been in Newfs practically all

of his life, growing up with the breed and eventually gaining the privilege of selecting a Newfoundland dog for the children of the island to present to the Duke and Duchess of Cornwall and York. He began his American breeding program under the Westerland name. In addition to producing outstanding dogs, he served as officers of both the now-defunct North American Newfoundland Club and the Newfoundland Club of America (NCA), which remains as the American Kennel Club parent club. Macpherson was active in the breed until his death in 1963.

The hardships of World War II produced a serious decline in the Newfoundland as it did in all pure-bred dogs. Although the working Newfoundland served admirably during the war under arduous conditions in Alaska and the Aleutian Islands, where they hauled supplies and ammunition for the Allied forces, serious fanciers in Newfoundland and other war-impoverished countries were unable to continue their breeding programs, and the number and quality of pure-bred stock declined and weakened.

However, the breed has always been able to withstand setbacks and today thrives thanks to dedicated breeders and fanciers. Although there had been a previous incarnation of the

THE FOUNDING THREE

It is believed that during the 1950s, every Newf champion bred in the United States was a descendant of Cabin Boy, Baron and Neptune, the three Siki offspring who were exported to America following World War II.

Newfoundland Club of America, established in 1914, today's NCA was established in 1930. Among this non-profit organization's activities are protecting correct type in the breed, emphasizing the Newf's talents and natural qualities, educating the public about the breed, researching health issues, setting down ethics for breeding and running a rescue network. With a stronghold in the US and such a dedicated following, the Newfoundland's future is secure.

There is no doubt the most famous fancier of the Newfoundland was the poet Lord Byron, who had this tribute inscribed on the monument on the grave of his beloved Newfoundland companion, Boatswain:

When some proud son of man returns to earth
Unknown to glory, but upheld by birth,
The sculptor's art exhausts the art of woe,
And storied urns record who rest below;

Not what he was, but what he should have been;
But the poor Dog, in life the firmest friend,
The first to welcome, foremost to defend;
Whose honest heart is still his master's own,
Who labours, fights, lives, breathes for him alone
Unhonor'd falls, unnoticed all his worth,
Denied in Heaven the soul he held on earth;
While man, vain insect! hopes to be forgiven,
And claims himself sole exclusive of Heaven!
Oh, man! Thou feeble tenant of an hour,
Debas'd by slavery, or corrupt by power,
Who knows thee well, must quit thee with disgust,
Degraded mass of animated dust!
Thy love is lust, thy friendship all a cheat,
Thy smiles hypocrisy, thy words deceit!
By nature vile, ennobled but by name,
Each kindred brute might bid thee blush for shame.
Ye! Who, perchance, behold this single Urn
Pass on—it honours none you wish to mourn;
To mark a Friend's remains these stones arise,
I never knew but one, and here he lies.

Byron then wrote the following famous epitaph to be inscribed on the side of the pedestal upon which Boatswain's urn rested:

Near this spot are deposited the remains of one who possessed beauty without vanity, strength without insolence, courage without ferocity and all the virtues of man without his vices.

This praise, which would be unmeaning flattery if inscribed over human ashes is but a just tribute to the memory of Boatswain, a dog who was born at Newfoundland in May 1803 and died at Newstead Abbey, England, in November 1808. Just imagine what Lord Byron might have inscribed had his beloved Boatswain lived for more than five-and-a half years!

Newfoundland as muse: The face and soul that inspired Lord Byron and other great poets to pen many exceptional verses.

The Newfoundland is an easy-to-live-with breed if you have enough space to properly accommodate him.

CHARACTERISTICS OF THE

NEWFOUNDLAND

IS THE NEWF RIGHT FOR YOU?
The Newfoundland is best known for his sweet and gentle disposition, and most especially for his great love of children and his protective feelings toward them. He is exceptionally tolerant of toddler behavior and the sort of rough-house activity that would disturb other breeds and cause them to leave, object or become aggressive. Because of his unswerving patience, the Newf can easily be victimized by a child, a situation that requires stringent parental supervision and intervention. The opposite can also be true, and children are often unintentionally hurt by their massive Newfie friend who is totally oblivious to his size and who inadvertently bumps or knocks over the child or slobbers all over him.

The Newfoundland can also be quite protective of adult family members as well as strangers. Stories abound about Newfies who have saved their human families or friends from life-threatening situations, with a great many of those exploits involving water rescues or other life-saving intervention by a Newfoundland.

The Newfoundland is an easy-to-live-with dog if you have the space and tolerance for an animal who will probably outweigh some family members, who will shed his heavy coat all over your house and who drools and may sling a bit of slobber when excited. "House-proud" is an expression often heard among breed fanciers. A fastidious housekeeper could not live successfully with typical Newfie habits as the hair and slobber would cause no end of anguish.

The Newfoundland requires frequent grooming to maintain a healthy coat and keep shedding to a minimum. He also needs regular exercise, consisting of brisk daily

Are you ready to share your heart, your home and even your bed with the Newfoundland?

walks as well as human attention and affection to prevent boredom, unhappiness and separation anxiety. You will need a bigger-than-average dog-food budget to support the Newfie's rapid growth during his first year.

The Newf coat goes through several stages of puppy growth before reaching its full adult color and texture at about 18 to 24 months of age. The longer guard hairs along the back appear at about four months of age along with shorter hair on the legs, feet and face. The true adult coat is apparent by the second year after one full shedding season. Coats can change dramatically during the maturation period, with the soft, straight fur's becoming coarse and wavy. Feathering on the legs and feet also continues to grow in

A furry giant with a heart of gold, the Newfie is a snuggler beyond compare.

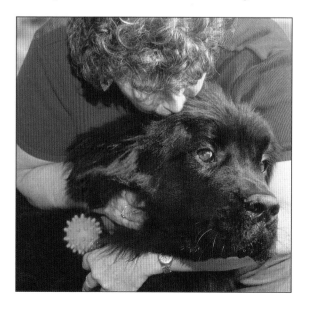

length and density during the first two or three years.

As with all giant-breed dogs, the Newfoundland matures slowly and is not fully grown until he is about three years old. Sadly, he is short-lived, with a lifespan of perhaps eight to ten years.

BREED-SPECIFIC HEALTH CONCERNS

HIP DYSPLASIA

Hip dysplasia (HD) is a developmental disease in which the ball-and-socket joint of the hip is poorly or abnormally formed. In dysplastic dogs, the "ball" (femoral head) does not fit properly into the "socket" (acetabulum). Dysplasia can affect one or both hips. A mild case of HD can cause pain and possibly arthritis, and a severe case can render a working dog worthless at his breed-specific task. Dogs who are mildly affected may not become symptomatic until later in life.

In the US, the Orthopedic Foundation for Animals (OFA) is the main body for the testing and grading of hips. X-rays are submitted and evaluated, and given one of the following classifications: Excellent, Good, Fair, Borderline, Mild, Moderate, Severe. The first three grades are considered "normal" and are issued an OFA number; dogs who score Borderline or lower should not be bred. It should be understood that while

HD is mainly considered to be genetic, it also can be influenced by nutrition, obesity and environmental factors. Nonetheless, selective breeding of dysplasia-free dogs is the first step in eradicating this debilitating condition.

The Newfoundland breed has a relatively high percentage of dysplasia; recent statistics show over 20% of the breed's showing some degree of dysplasia. However, the number of dysplastic dogs has steadily been on the decrease over the past three decades. Therefore, the Newf's health has improved due to the efforts of responsible breeders, and the future looks bright.

HEART CONDITIONS

Sub-valvular aortic stenosis (SAS) is an abnormality of the heart in which the aortic valve develops fibrous tissue, causing a narrowing (stenosis) of the valve and thus restricting the blood flow through the valve. In the worst-case scenario, an affected dog may collapse and die suddenly, without warning.

Pups should be checked for detectable heart murmurs by a vet before leaving the breeder, although final evaluation is done at one year of age by a veterinary cardiologist. Of course, any dog diagnosed with SAS should *not* be bred.

Newfoundlands are also recorded as having three other heart conditions: pulmonic stenosis, which is a narrowing of the pulmonic valve; patent ductus arteriosus, a condition in which an in-utero bypass blood vessel fails to shut off after the pup is whelped; and tricuspid valvular dysplasia, a condition similar to blue babies in humans. Although not common in the breed, they are sufficiently serious to warrant examination by a veterinary cardiologist. Affected dogs should never be bred.

CYSTINURIA

This condition affects dogs whose bodies cannot normally absorb the

Newfoundland and owner have no trouble seeing eye-to-eye— literally!

The Newfoundland is noble and massive, impressing all who see him with strength, dignity and athleticism.

implemented. The outlook is good and eventual eradication of the disease is possible if breeders are diligent in screening their breeding stock and eliminating all affected dogs from breeding programs.

GASTRIC DILATATION-VOLVULUS (GDV)

Gastric dilatation-volvulus, also known as gastric torsion, and more commonly referred to as bloat, is a life-threatening condition that most often occurs in deep-chested breeds like Newfoundlands, Boxers, Great Danes and several other large breeds. The stomach of the animal, quite suddenly and for no apparent reason, fills with gas and begins to twist, cutting off the blood supply to the animal's vital organs, causing shock and death within a matter of hours. Immediate veterinary intervention is necessary if the dog is to survive.

amino acid cystine. In this case, cystine forms crystals in the urine, which can further form kidney and bladder stones. These stones (calculi) can cause serious illness, even completely blocking the flow of urine, which can cause many complications to the bladder and kidneys. In the most severe cases, death can result. While this condition is not unique to the Newfoundland, the breed is affected by the most severe type of cystinuria.

Symptoms include recurrent urinary tract disorder, unproductive attempts to pass urine or passing urine with blood. This problem has only been discovered in the Newf fairly recently, but its genetic basis has been determined and a testing scheme has been

The cause of bloat remains unknown, although it is thought that the risk can be minimized by feeding several small meals instead of one or two large meals and limiting exercise before and after eating. Although bloat is not a heritable disease, the condition is common enough in large-breed dogs that a wise owner will familiarize himself with preventative measures, as well as the physical symptoms and proper emergency care in the event it should occur.

DO YOU KNOW ABOUT HIP DYSPLASIA?

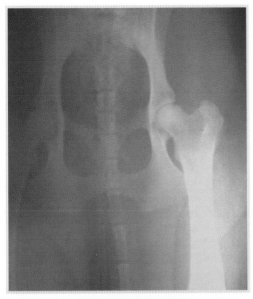

X-ray of a dog with "Good" hips.

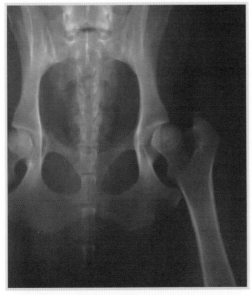

X-ray of a dog with "Moderate" dysplastic hips.

Hip dysplasia is a fairly common condition found in pure-bred dogs. When a dog has hip dysplasia, his hind leg has an incorrectly formed hip joint. By constant use of the hip joint, it becomes more and more loose, wears abnormally and may become arthritic.

Hip dysplasia can only be confirmed with an x-ray, but certain symptoms may indicate a problem. Your dog may have a hip dysplasia problem if he walks in a peculiar manner, hops instead of smoothly runs, uses his hind legs in unison (to keep the pressure off the weak joint), has trouble getting up from a prone position or always sits with both legs together on one side of his body.

As the dog matures, he may adapt well to life with a bad hip, but in a few years the arthritis develops and many dogs with hip dysplasia become crippled.

Hip dysplasia is considered an inherited disease and only can be diagnosed definitively by x-ray when the dog is two years old, although symptoms often appear earlier. Some experts claim that a special diet might help your puppy outgrow the bad hip, but the usual treatments are surgical. The removal of the pectineus muscle, the removal of the round part of the femur, reconstructing the pelvis and replacing the hip with an artificial one are all surgical interventions that are expensive, but they are usually very successful. Follow the advice of your veterinarian.

NEWFOUNDLAND

INTRODUCTION TO THE BREED STANDARD

A breed standard is quite simply a guideline, a detailed description that outlines what an ideal specimen of a given breed should look and act like. Standards, as originally agreed upon by the breed fanciers who devised them, are intended to be a guideline and, as such, are subject to much interpretation. Breed judges use the standard as their yardstick when deciding upon the merits of a show dog, selecting what they believe to be the best representative of that breed. The goal is for only the best to win and be bred from, thereby preserving qualities only from the worthiest specimens of the breed. Quite often the human element intervenes, and individual interpretations and preferences disrupt the process, which can affect the function and form of future generations of the breed.

The standard for the Newfoundland defines the basic requirements for a large breed of dog with natural life-saving instincts, a gentle temperament and sound and active movement.

Although it is surely impossible for a judge to know if the dog he is observing is capable of swimming or rescuing a human from a frigid sea, a hands-on examination of the dog's muscle tone should identify the difference between working and non-working condition.

Temperament is of utmost importance in the Newf, and any display of growling or nervous behavior should be heavily penalized, as it is not in keeping with the true character of the breed.

Solid black is the dominant color of the Newfoundland, and the Landseer black-and-white is recessive to the solid black color gene. Solid bronze is also recessive to black, and the solid gray is a dilute of the black. The Landseer black on a white background is allowed by the standard. However, if the Landseer is bred with a dog with brown or gray backgrounds, a bronze-and-white or a gray-and-white dog may result. Both combinations are disqualifications, according to the standard.

THE AMERICAN KENNEL CLUB BREED STANDARD FOR THE NEWFOUNDLAND

General Appearance: The Newfoundland is a sweet-dispositioned dog that acts neither dull nor ill-tempered. He is a devoted companion. A multipurpose dog, at home on land and in water, the Newfoundland is capable of draft work and possesses natural life-saving abilities.

The Newfoundland is a large, heavily coated, well balanced dog that is deep-bodied, heavily boned, muscular, and strong. A good specimen of the breed has dignity and proud head carriage. The following description is that of the ideal Newfoundland. Any

deviation from this ideal is to be penalized to the extent of the deviation. Structural and movement faults common to all work-

The solid black and solid brown Newfoundlands represent two color possibilities in the breed.

Genetically speaking, solid black is the dominant color in the breed with the Landseer (black-and-white) being recessive.

ing dogs are as undesirable in the Newfoundland as in any other breed, even though they are not specifically mentioned herein.

Size, Proportion, Substance: Average height for adult dogs is 28 inches, for adult bitches, 26 inches. Approximate weight of adult dogs ranges from 130 to 150 pounds, adult bitches from 100 to 120 pounds. The dog's appearance is more massive throughout than the bitch's. Large size is desirable, but never at the expense of balance, structure, and correct gait. The Newfoundland is slightly longer than tall when measured from the point of shoulder to point of buttocks and from withers to ground. He is a dog of considerable substance which is determined by spring of rib, strong muscle, and heavy bone.

As is common in most breeds of dog, the scissors bite is desirable.

Head: The head is massive, with a broad *skull*, slightly arched crown, and strongly developed occipital bone. Cheeks are well developed. *Eyes* are dark brown. (Browns and Grays may have lighter eyes and should be penalized only to the extent that color affects expression.) They are relatively small, deep-set, and spaced wide apart. Eyelids fit closely with no inversion. *Ears* are relatively small and triangular with rounded tips. They are set on the skull level with, or slightly above, the brow and lie close to the head. When the ear is brought forward, it reaches to the inner corner of the eye on the same side. *Expression* is soft and reflects the characteristics of the breed: benevolence, intelligence, and dignity.

Forehead and face are smooth and free of wrinkles. Slope of the stop is moderate but, because of the well developed brow, it may appear abrupt in profile. The *muzzle* is clean-cut, broad throughout its length, and deep. Depth and length are approximately equal, the length from tip of nose to stop being less than that from stop to occiput. The top of the muzzle is rounded, and the bridge, in profile, is straight or only slightly arched. Teeth meet in a scissors or level *bite*. Dropped lower incisors, in an otherwise normal bite, are not indicative of a skeletal malocclusion and should be considered only a minor deviation.

Neck, Topline, Body: The *neck* is strong and well set on the shoulders and is long enough for proud head carriage. The *back* is strong, broad, and muscular and is level from just behind the withers to the croup. The chest is full and deep with the brisket reaching at least down to the elbows. Ribs are well sprung, with the anterior third of the rib cage tapered to allow elbow clearance. The flank is deep. The croup is broad and slopes slightly. *Tail*—Tail set follows the natural line of the croup. The tail is broad at the base and strong. It has no kinks, and the distal bone reaches to the hock. When the dog is standing relaxed, its tail hangs straight or with a slight curve at the end. When the dog is in motion or excited, the tail is carried out, but it does not curl over the back.

Forequarters: Shoulders are muscular and well laid back.

Head study in profile, showing correct type, structure, proportion and size.

Elbows lie directly below the highest point of the withers. Forelegs are muscular, heavily boned, straight, and parallel to each other, and the elbows point directly to the rear. The distance from elbow to ground equals about half the dog's height. Pasterns are strong and slightly sloping. Feet are proportionate to the body in size, webbed, and cat foot in type. Dewclaws may be removed.

FAULTS IN PROFILE
Left: Upright shoulders, high in the rear, lacking angulation in the rear, long back.
Right: Short neck, upright shoulders, lacking adequate bone, weak pasterns, flat feet, sloping topline, weak rear.

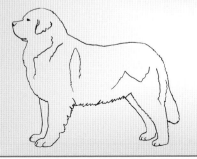
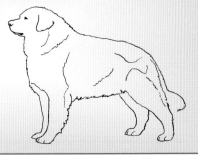

Dog in profile, showing correct type, balance, structure and substance with mature coat.

front feet. Dewclaws should be removed.

Coat: The adult Newfoundland has a flat, water-resistant, double coat that tends to fall back into place when rubbed against the nap. The outer coat is coarse, moderately long, and full, either straight or with a wave. The undercoat is soft and dense, although it is often less dense during the summer months or in warmer climates. Hair on the face and muzzle is short and fine. The backs of the legs are feathered all the way down. The tail is covered with long dense hair. Excess hair may be trimmed for neatness. Whiskers need not be trimmed.

Hindquarters: The rear assembly is powerful, muscular, and heavily boned. Viewed from the rear, the legs are straight and parallel. Viewed from the side, the thighs are broad and fairly long. Stifles and hocks are well bent and the line from hock to ground is perpendicular. Hocks are well let down. Hind feet are similar to the

Color: Color is secondary to type, structure, and soundness. Recognized Newfoundland colors are black, brown, gray, and white and black.

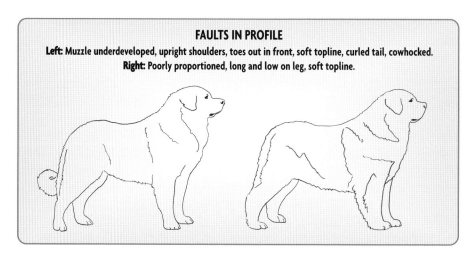

FAULTS IN PROFILE
Left: Muzzle underdeveloped, upright shoulders, toes out in front, soft topline, curled tail, cowhocked.
Right: Poorly proportioned, long and low on leg, soft topline.

Solid Colors—Blacks, Browns, and Grays may appear as solid colors or solid colors with white at any, some, or all, of the following locations: chin, chest, toes, and tip of tail. Any amount of white found at these locations is typical and is not penalized. Also typical are a tinge of bronze on a black or gray coat and lighter furnishings on a brown or gray coat. *Landseer*—White base coat with black markings. Typically, the head is solid black, or black with white on the muzzle, with or without a blaze. There is a separate black saddle and black on the rump extending onto a white tail. Markings, on either Solid Colors or Landseers, might deviate considerably from those described and should be penalized only to the extent of the deviation. Clear white or white with minimal ticking is preferred. Beauty of markings should be considered only when comparing dogs of otherwise comparable quality and never at the expense of type, structure and soundness. *Disqualifications*—Any colors or combinations of colors not specifically described are disqualified.

Gait: The Newfoundland in motion has good reach, strong drive, and gives the impression of effortless power. His gait is smooth and rhythmic, covering the maximum amount of ground with the minimum number of steps.

This brown Newfoundland is winning the Group at an FCI show.

Forelegs and hind legs travel straight forward. As the dog's speed increases, the legs tend toward single tracking. When moving, a slight roll of the skin is characteristic of the breed. Essential to good movement is the balance of correct front and rear assemblies.

Temperament: Sweetness of temperament is the hallmark of the Newfoundland; this is the most important single characteristic of the breed.

Disqualifications: *Any colors or combinations of colors not specifically described are disqualified.*

Approved May 8, 1990
Effective June 28, 1990

NEWFOUNDLAND

PUPPY APPEARANCE

Your puppy should have a well-fed appearance but not a distended abdomen, which may indicate worms or incorrect feeding, or both. The body should be firm, with a solid feel. The skin of the abdomen should be pale pink and clean, without signs of scratching or rash. Check the hind legs to make certain that dewclaws were removed, if any were present at birth.

SELECTING THE PERFECT PUPPY

The first step in finding a good pup is finding a reputable breeder. Responsible breeders screen their breeding stock for genetic defects and know how to build a pedigree that will produce quality pups. Their pups are raised and socialized in a clean, safe environment. Such breeders spend countless hours with their Newfie babies and know the differences between each pup, things like their levels of confidence, dominance, attitude and who snuggles best. Good breeders can also offer insight into which pup will best achieve your goals, whether you plan to train your Newf for the show ring, obedience competition or water skills, or just enjoy him as a lovable family companion.

If you are convinced that the Newfoundland is the ideal dog for you, it's time to learn about where to find a puppy and what to look for. Locating a litter of Newfs should not present a problem for the new owner. You should inquire about breeders in your region who enjoy a good reputation in the breed. You are looking for an established breeder with outstanding dog ethics and a strong commitment to the breed. New owners should have as many questions as they have doubts. An established breeder is indeed the one to answer your four million questions and make you comfortable with your choice of the Newfoundland. An established breeder will sell you a puppy at a fair price if, and only if, the breeder determines that you are a suitable, worthy owner of his dogs. An established breeder can be relied upon for advice, no matter what time of day or night. A reputable breeder will accept a puppy back, without questions, should you decide that this is not the right dog for you.

When choosing a breeder, reputation is much more important than convenience of location. Do not be overly impressed by breeders who run brag advertisements in the dog presses about their stupendous champions. The real quality breeders are quiet and unassuming. You hear about them at dog shows and trials, by word of mouth. You may be well advised to avoid the novice who lives only a few miles away. The local novice breeder, trying so hard to get rid of that first litter of puppies, is more than accommodating and anxious to sell you one. That breeder will charge you as much

ARE YOU PREPARED?

Unfortunately, when a puppy is bought by someone who does not take into consideration the time and attention that dog ownership requires, it is the puppy who suffers when he is either abandoned or placed in a shelter by a frustrated owner. So all of the "homework" you do in preparation for your pup's arrival will benefit you both. The more informed you are, the more you will know what to expect and the better equipped you will be to handle the ups and downs of raising a puppy. Hopefully, everyone in the household is willing to do his part in raising and caring for the pup. The anticipation of owning a dog often brings a lot of promises from excited family members: "I will walk him every day," "I will feed him," "I will house-train him," etc., but these things take time and effort, and promises can easily be forgotten once the novelty of the new pet has worn off.

as any established breeder. The novice breeder isn't going to interrogate you and your family about your intentions with the puppy, the environment and training you can provide, etc. That breeder will be nowhere to be found when your poorly bred, badly adjusted four-pawed monster starts to growl and spit up at midnight or attempt to eat the family cat!

Choosing a breeder is an important first step in dog ownership. Fortunately, the majority of Newfoundland breeders is devoted to the breed and its well-being. New owners should have little problem finding a reputable breeder in their home state or region. The American Kennel Club is able to refer you to breeders of quality Newfoundlands, as can the Newfoundland Club of America (www.newfdogclub.org) and its regional clubs. Potential owners are encouraged to attend dog shows or trials to see Newfound-

> **A HEALTHY PUP**
> You should not even think about buying a puppy that looks sick, under-nourished, overly frightened or nervous. Sometimes a timid puppy will warm up to you after a 30-minute "let's-get-acquainted" session.

lands in action, to meet the owners and handlers firsthand and to get an idea of what Newfs look like outside a photographer's lens. Provided you approach the handlers when they are not busy with the dogs, most are more than willing to answer questions, recommend breeders and give advice.

Once you have contacted and met a breeder or two and made your choice about which breeder is best suited to your needs, it is time to visit the litter. Keep in mind that many top breeders have waiting lists. Sometimes new owners have to wait a year or more for a puppy. If you are really committed to the breeder whom you've selected, then you will wait (and hope for an early arrival!). If not, you may have to go with your second- or third-choice breeder. Don't be too anxious, however. If the breeder doesn't have a waiting list, or any customers, there is probably a good reason. It's no different than visiting a restaurant with no clientele. The better establish-

When selecting a Newfoundland, an owner must decide on one of the breed's color possibilities, each of which is duly handsome and sought after.

It is best to see the mother with her puppies so you can appreciate the inheritance of character, personality and physical traits in her offspring.

their puppies to leave early are more interested in making a profit than in their puppies' well-being. Puppies need to learn the rules of the pack from their dams, and most dams continue teaching the pups manners and dos and don'ts until around the eighth week. Breeders spend significant amounts of time with the Newfoundland toddlers so that they are able to interact with the "other species," i.e. humans. Given the long history that dogs and humans have, bonding between the two species is natural but must be nurtured. A

Like a pup to water! Living up to his water-dog heritage, this pup can't help but get his paws wet!

ments always have waiting lists—and it's usually worth the wait. Besides, isn't a puppy more important than a fancy meal?

Since you are likely to be choosing a Newfoundland as a pet dog and not a show or work-ing dog, you simply should select a pup that is friendly and attractive. Newfoundlands gener-ally have large litters, averaging six to ten puppies, so selection can be quite overwhelming once you have located a desirable litter. This is part of the great fun of selecting a Newfie puppy.

Breeders commonly allow visitors to see the litter by around the fifth or sixth week, and puppies leave for their new homes between the eighth and tenth week. Breeders who permit

"YOU BETTER SHOP AROUND!"

Finding a reputable breeder who sells healthy pups is very important, but make sure that the breeder you choose is not only someone you respect but also someone with whom you feel comfortable. Your breeder will be a resource long after you buy your puppy, and you must be able to call with reasonable questions without being made to feel like a pest! If you don't connect on a personal level, investigate some other breeders before making a final decision.

If the breeder from whom you are buying a puppy asks you a lot of personal questions, do not be insulted. Such a breeder wants to be sure that you will be a fit provider for his puppy.

well-bred, well-socialized Newfoundland pup wants nothing more than to be near you and please you.

COMMITMENT OF OWNERSHIP
After considering all of these factors, you have most likely already made some very important decisions about selecting

YOUR SCHEDULE . . .

If you lead an erratic, unpredictable life, with daily or weekly changes in your work requirements, consider the problems of owning a puppy. The new puppy has to be fed regularly, socialized (loved, petted, handled, introduced to other people) and, most importantly, allowed to visit outdoors for toilet training. As the dog gets older, he can be more tolerant of deviations in his feeding and toilet relief.

your puppy. You have chosen the Newfoundland, which means that you have decided which characteristics you want in a dog and what type of dog will best fit into your family and lifestyle. If you have selected a breeder, you have gone a step further—you have done your research and found a responsible, conscientious person who breeds quality Newfoundlands and who should be a reliable source of help as you and your puppy adjust to life together. If you have observed a litter in action, you have obtained a firsthand look at the dynamics of a puppy "pack" and, thus, you should have learned about each pup's individual personality—perhaps you have even found one that particularly appeals to you.

However, even if you have not yet found the Newfoundland puppy of your dreams, observing

Your choice of a Newf means adding a loyal and loving canine companion to the family.

ber, though, you cannot be too careful when it comes to deciding on the type of dog you want and finding out about your prospective pup's background. Buying a puppy is not—or *should* not be—just another whimsical purchase. This is one instance in which you actually

A yard with a sturdy fence that can contain a large, strong dog is an ideal place for the Newf to exercise.

pups will help you learn to recognize certain behavior and to determine what a pup's behavior indicates about his temperament. You will be able to pick out which pups are the leaders, which ones are less outgoing, which ones are confident, which ones are shy, playful, friendly, aggressive, etc. Equally as important, you will learn to recognize what a healthy pup should look and act like. All of these things will help you in your search, and when you find the Newfoundland that was meant for you, you will know it!

Researching your breed, selecting a responsible breeder and observing as many pups as possible are all important steps on the way to dog ownership. It may seem like a lot of effort...and you have not even taken the pup home yet! Remem-

PEDIGREE VS. REGISTRATION CERTIFICATE

Too often new owners are confused between these two important documents. Your puppy's pedigree, essentially a family tree, is a written record of a dog's genealogy of three generations or more. The pedigree will show you the names as well as performance titles of all dogs in your pup's background. Your breeder must provide you with a registration application, with his part properly filled out. You must complete the application and send it to the AKC with the proper fee. Every puppy must come from a litter that has been AKC-registered by the breeder, born in the USA and from a sire and dam that are also registered with the AKC.

The seller must provide you with complete records to identify the puppy. The AKC requires that the seller provide the buyer with the following: breed; sex, color and markings; date of birth; litter number (when available); names and registration numbers of the parents; breeder's name; and date sold or delivered.

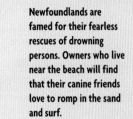

Newfoundlands are famed for their fearless rescues of drowning persons. Owners who live near the beach will find that their canine friends love to romp in the sand and surf.

"SMILE"

The Newfoundland will occasionally "smile," displaying his teeth and gums in a wide grin. Contrary to those who interpret the look as a sign of aggression, the "grin" is actually a Newfie's way of showing his submission, expecially when he thinks he has been naughty.

do get to choose your own family! You may be thinking that buying a puppy should be fun—it should not be so serious and so much work. Keep in mind that your puppy is not a cuddly stuffed toy or decorative lawn ornament, but a creature that will become a real (and a really *big*) member of your family. You will come to realize that, while buying a puppy is a pleasurable and exciting endeavor, it is not something to be taken lightly.

Relax...the fun will start when the pup comes home!

Always keep in mind that a puppy is nothing more than a baby in a furry disguise...a baby who is virtually helpless in a human world and who trusts his owner for fulfillment of his basic needs for survival. In addition to food, water and shelter, your pup needs care, protection, guidance and love. If you are not prepared to commit to this, then you are not prepared to own a dog.

Wait a minute, you say. How hard could this be? All of my neighbors own dogs and they seem to be doing just fine. Why should I have to worry about all of this? Well, you should not worry about it; in fact, you will probably find that once your Newfoundland pup gets used to his new home, he will fall into his place in the family quite naturally. But it never hurts to emphasize the commitment of dog ownership. With some time and patience, it is really not too difficult to raise a curious and exuberant Newfoundland pup to be a well-adjusted and well-mannered adult dog—a dog that could be your most loyal friend.

PREPARING PUPPY'S PLACE IN YOUR HOME

Researching your breed and finding a breeder are only two aspects of the "homework" you will have to do before taking your Newfoundland puppy home. You will also have to prepare your home and family for the new addition. Much as you would prepare a nursery for a newborn baby, you will need to designate a place in your home that will be the puppy's own. How you prepare your home will depend on how much freedom the dog will be allowed. Whatever you decide, you must ensure that he has a place that he can call his own.

When you bring your new puppy into your home, you are bringing him into what will become his home as well. Obviously, you did not buy a puppy so that he could take control and "rule the roost" in your home, but in order for a puppy to grow into a stable, well-adjusted dog, he has to feel comfortable in his surroundings. Remember, he is leaving the warmth and security of his mother and littermates, as

It's easy to see the "Bear Dog" in today's Newfoundland.

well as the familiarity of the only place he has ever known, so it is important to make his transition as easy as possible. By preparing a place in your home for the puppy, you are making him feel as welcome as possible in a strange new place. It should not take him long to get used to it, but the sudden shock of being transplanted is somewhat traumatic for a young pup. Imagine how a small child would feel in the same situation—that is how your puppy must be feeling. It is up to you to reassure him and to let him know, "Little Newfie, you are going to like it here!"

INHERIT THE MIND

In order to know whether or not a puppy will fit into your lifestyle, you need to assess his personality. A good way to do this is to interact with his parents. Your pup inherits not only his appearance but also his temperament from the sire and dam. If the parents are fearful or aggressive, traits not typical in the Newf, these same traits may likely show up in your puppy.

When bringing your new Newf puppy into your home, you are welcoming him into your life. Make the puppy feel comfortable in his new surroundings.

PUPPY PERSONALITY

When a litter becomes available to you, choosing a pup out of all those adorable faces will not be an easy task! Sound temperament is of utmost importance, but each pup has his own personality and some may be better suited to you than others. A feisty, independent pup will do well in a home with older children and adults, while quiet, shy puppies will thrive in homes with minimal noise and distractions. Your breeder knows the pups best and should be able to guide you in the right direction.

WHAT YOU SHOULD BUY

CRATE

To someone unfamiliar with the use of crates in dog training, it may seem like punishment to shut a dog in a crate, but this is not the case at all. More and more breeders and trainers around the world are recommending crates as preferred tools for show puppies and pet puppies alike. Crates are not cruel—crates have many humane and highly effective uses in dog care and training. For example, crate training is a very popular and very successful housebreaking method, a crate can keep your dog safe during travel and, perhaps most importantly, a crate provides your dog with a place of his own in your home. It serves as a "doggie bedroom" of sorts—your Newfoundland can curl up in his crate when he wants to sleep or when he just needs a break. Many dogs sleep in their crates overnight. With soft bedding and his favorite toy, a crate becomes a cozy pseudo-den for your dog. Like his ances-

Even a massive dog like the Newf starts out as a tiny puppy, completely dependent on his owner for care, love and guidance as he grows up.

PHOTO COURTESY OF DOSKOCIL.

or fiberglass. There are advantages and disadvantages to each type. For example, a wire crate is more open, allowing the air to flow through and affording the dog a view of what is going on around him, while a fiberglass crate is sturdier. Both can double as travel crates, providing protection for the dog in the car.

The size of the crate is another thing to consider. Puppies do not stay puppies forever—in fact, sometimes it seems as if they grow right before your eyes. The Newf puppy grows rapidly, and unless

Your local pet shop may not have in stock a crate large enough for a fully grown Newfoundland, so a special order may be required.

tors, he too will seek out the comfort and retreat of a den—you just happen to be providing him with something a little more luxurious than what his early ancestors enjoyed.

As far as purchasing a crate, the type that you buy is up to you. It will most likely be one of the two most popular types: wire

CRATE-TRAINING TIPS

During crate training, you should partition off the section of the crate in which the pup stays. If he is given too big an area, this will hinder your training efforts. Crate training is based on the fact that a dog does not like to soil his sleeping quarters, so it is ineffective to keep a pup in an area that is so big that he can eliminate in one end and get far enough away from it to sleep. Also, you want to make the crate den-like for the pup. Blankets and a favorite toy will make the crate cozy for the small pup; as he grows, you may want to evict some of his "roommates" to make more room. It will take some coaxing at first, but be patient. Given some time to get used to it, your pup will adapt to his new home-within-a-home quite nicely.

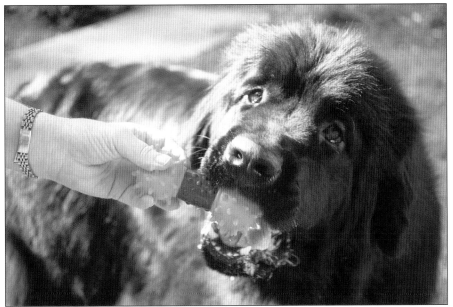

Big dogs need big toys. Purchase sturdy toys, made for large breeds, without small pieces that may be broken off or swallowed.

you have the money and the inclination to buy a new crate every time your pup has a growth spurt, it is better to get one that will accommodate your dog both as a pup and at full size. A giant-size crate will be necessary for a full-grown Newfoundland, a crate that measures about 48 by 30 inches and allows him to stand fully and lie down comfortably.

BEDDING
A soft lambswool pad in the dog's crate will help him feel more at home, and you may also like to put a small blanket in the crate. These things will take the place of the leaves, twigs, etc., that the pup would use in the wild to make a den; the pup can make his own "burrow" in the crate. Although your pup is far removed from his den-making ancestors, the denning instinct is still a part of his genetic makeup. Second, until you take your pup home, he has been sleeping amid the warmth of his mother and litter-mates, and while a blanket is not

---

MENTAL AND DENTAL
Toys not only help your puppy get the physical and mental stimulation he needs but also provide a great way to keep his teeth clean. Hard rubber or nylon toys, especially those constructed with grooves, are designed to scrape away plaque, preventing bad breath and gum infection.

PLAY'S THE THING

Teaching the puppy to play with his toys in running and fetching games is an ideal way to help the puppy develop muscle, learn motor skills and bond with you, his owner and master. He also needs to learn how to inhibit his bite reflex and never to use his teeth on people, forbidden objects and other animals in play. Whenever you play with your puppy, you make the rules. This becomes an important message to your puppy in teaching him that you are the pack leader and control everything he does in life. Once your dog accepts you as his leader, your relationship with him will be cemented for life.

the same as a warm, breathing body, it still provides heat and something with which to snuggle. You will want to wash your pup's bedding frequently in case he has an accident in his crate, and replace or remove any blanket or padding that becomes ragged and starts to fall apart.

Toys

Toys are a must for dogs of all ages, especially for curious playful pups. Puppies are the "children" of the dog world, and what child does not love toys? Chew toys provide enjoyment for both dog and owner—your dog will enjoy playing with his favorite toys, while you will enjoy the fact that they distract him from your expensive shoes and leather sofa. Puppies love to chew; in fact, chewing is a physical need for pups as they are teething, and everything looks appetizing! The full range of your possessions— from old dish towel to Oriental carpet—are fair game in the eyes of a teething pup. Puppies are not all that discerning when it comes to finding something to literally "sink their teeth into"— everything tastes great!

Newfoundland puppies are fairly devoted chewers since they have retrieving instincts and are quite fixated on "all things oral." Therefore, only the strongest toys, of appropriate size for the growing pup, should be offered to them. As your puppy matures, he will require larger toys; adult Newfs require the largest size available.

Breeders advise owners to resist stuffed toys, because they can become de-stuffed in no

time. The overly excited pup may ingest the stuffing, which is neither nutritious nor digestible. Similarly, squeaky toys are quite popular, but must be avoided for the Newfoundland. Perhaps a squeaky toy can be used as an aid in training, but not for free play. Monitor the condition of all of your pup's toys carefully and get rid of any that have been chewed to the point of becoming potentially dangerous.

Be careful of natural bones, which have a tendency to splinter into sharp, dangerous pieces. Also be careful of rawhide, which can turn into pieces that are easy to swallow or become a mushy mess on your carpet.

LEAD

A nylon lead is probably the best option as it is the most resistant to puppy teeth should your pup take a liking to chewing on his lead. Of course, this is a habit that should be nipped in the bud, but, if your

TOYS, TOYS, TOYS!

With a big variety of dog toys available, and so many that look like they would be a lot of fun for a dog, be careful in your selection. It is amazing what a set of puppy teeth can do to an innocent-looking toy, so, obviously, safety is a major consideration. Be sure to choose the most durable products that you can find. Hard nylon bones and toys are a safe bet, and many of them are offered in different scents and flavors that will be sure to capture your dog's attention. It is always fun to play a game of fetch with your dog, and there are balls and flying discs that are specially made to withstand dog teeth.

A friendly tug-of-war among a trio of Newfs. Strong rope toys are enjoyed by dogs, with the added benefit of acting like floss as they chew, helping to keep teeth clean.

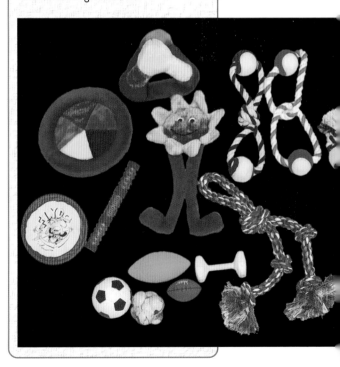

Your local pet
shop will have
a variety of
leads from
which you can
choose the
one best
suited to your
Newfie. You
will need a
strong, but
not too heavy,
lead.

pup likes to chew on his lead, he has a very slim chance of being able to chew through the strong nylon. Nylon leads are also light-weight, which is good for a young Newfoundland who is just getting used to the idea of walking on a lead. For everyday walking and safety purposes, the nylon lead is a good choice. Once your Newf has grown, you will need a strong leather or chain lead to control up to 150 pounds of dog on the other end of your arm.

Collar

Your pup should get used to wearing a collar all the time since you will want to attach his ID tags to it; plus, you have to attach the lead to something! A lightweight nylon collar is a good choice; make sure that it fits snugly enough so that the

pup cannot wriggle out of it, but is loose enough so that it will not be uncomfortably tight around the pup's neck, taking his dense coat into consideration. You should be able to fit two fingers between the pup and the collar. It may take some time for your pup to get used to wearing the collar, but soon he will not even notice that it is there. Of course, your adult Newf requires a large collar, of appropriate thickness according to the lead you are using. Use of a choke collar is not suggested; a "gentle leader" or harness is more effective for a Newf that requires extra control.

Food and Water Bowls

Your pup will need two bowls, one for food and one for water.

FINANCIAL RESPONSIBILITY

Grooming tools, collars, leashes, a crate, a dog bed and, of course, toys will be expenses to you when you first obtain your pup, and the cost will continue throughout your dog's life-time. If your puppy damages or destroys your possessions (as most puppies surely will!) or something belonging to a neighbor, you can calcu-late additional expense. There is also flea and pest control, which every dog owner faces more than once. You must be able to handle the financial respon-sibility of owning a dog.

CHOOSE AN APPROPRIATE COLLAR

The **BUCKLE COLLAR** is the standard collar used for everyday purposes. Be sure that you adjust the buckle on growing puppies. Check it every day. It can become too tight overnight! These collars can be made of leather or nylon. Attach your dog's identification tags to this collar.

The **CHOKE COLLAR** is designed for training. It is constructed of highly polished steel so that it slides easily through the stainless steel loop. The idea is that the dog controls the pressure around his neck and he will stop pulling if the collar becomes uncomfortable. It is neither necessary nor recommended to use a choke collar with the gentle Newf.

The **HALTER** is for a trained dog that has to be restrained to prevent running away, chasing a cat and the like. Considered the most humane of all collars, it is frequently used on smaller dogs on which collars are not comfortable.

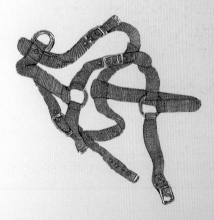

Your local pet shop sells an array of bowls for water and food. You will require large bowls, plus stands on which to elevate them, for your Newfie.

PHOTO COURTESY OF MIKKI PET PRODUCTS.

You may want two sets of bowls, one for inside and one for outside, depending on where the dog will be fed and where he will be spending time. Purchase the largest-size bowls that your pet shop offers. Stainless steel or sturdy plastic bowls are popular choices. Plastic bowls are more chewable, but dogs tend not to chew on the steel variety, which can be sterilized. It is important to buy sturdy bowls since anything is in danger of being chewed by puppy teeth and you do not want your dog to be constantly chewing apart his bowl (for his safety and for your wallet!). Purchasing bowl stands on which to elevate your Newf's bowls should be considered mandatory as a preventative measure against the potentially deadly bloat.

CLEANING SUPPLIES

Until a pup is house-trained, you will be doing a lot of cleaning. "Accidents" will occur, which is acceptable in the beginning because the puppy does not know any better. All you can do is be prepared to clean up any accidents. Old rags, towels, newspapers and a safe disinfectant are good to have on hand.

BEYOND THE BASICS

The items previously discussed are the bare necessities. You will find out what else you need as you go along—grooming

TOXIC PLANTS

Many plants can be toxic to dogs. If you see your dog carrying a piece of vegetation in his mouth, approach him in a quiet, disinterested manner, avoid eye contact, pet him and gradually remove the plant from his mouth. Alternatively, offer him a treat and maybe he'll drop the plant on his own accord. Be sure no toxic plants are growing in your own yard or kept in your home.

It is your responsibility to clean up after your Newfoundland. Tools are available to make cleaning up less of a chore.

supplies, flea/tick protection, baby gates to partition a room, etc. These things will vary depending on your situation, but it is important that right away

you have everything you need to feed and make your Newfoundland comfortable in his first few days at home.

PUPPY-PROOFING YOUR HOME

Aside from making sure that your Newfoundland will be comfortable in your home, you also have to make sure that your home is safe for your Newfoundland. This means taking precautions that your pup will not get into anything he should not get into and that there is nothing within his reach that may harm him should he sniff it, chew it, inspect it, etc. This probably

Puppies will attempt to chew on anything they can find. Keep a close eye on your Newf puppy to make sure that he doesn't make a "toy" out of something that can harm him.

NATURAL TOXINS

Examine your grass and landscaping before bringing your puppy home. Many varieties of plants have leaves, stems or flowers that are toxic if ingested, and you can depend on a curious puppy to investigate them. Ask your vet for information on poisonous plants or research them at your library.

within the house, keep any potentially dangerous items in the "off-limits" areas. An electrical cord can pose a danger should the puppy decide to taste it—and who is going to convince a pup that it would not make a great chew toy? Cords should be fastened tightly against the wall, out of puppy's sight and reach. If your dog is going to spend time in a crate, make sure that there is nothing near his crate that he can reach if he sticks his curious little nose or paws through the openings. Just as you would with

A happy giant-dog home! Your yard must be securely fenced to create a safe, escape-proof place for your Newf.

seems obvious since, while you are primarily concerned with your pup's safety, at the same time you do not want your belongings to be ruined.

Breakables should be placed out of reach if your dog is to have full run of the house. If he is to be limited to certain places a child, keep all household cleaners and chemicals where the pup cannot reach them.

It is also important to make sure that the outside of your home is safe. Of course, your puppy should never be unsupervised, but a pup let loose in the yard will want to run and explore, and he should be granted that freedom. Do not let a fence give you a false sense of security; you would be surprised how crafty (and persistent) a dog can be in working out how to dig under a fence and squeeze his way through holes, or to jump or climb over a fence. The remedy is to make the fence well embedded into the ground and high enough so that it really is impossible for your dog to get over it (about 6 feet should suffice). Be sure to secure any gaps in the fence. Check the fence periodically to ensure that it is in good shape and make repairs as needed; a very determined pup may return to the same spot to "work on it" until he is able to get through, around or over.

FIRST TRIP TO THE VET

You have selected your puppy, and your home and family are ready. Now all you have to do is collect your Newfoundland from the breeder and the fun begins, right? Well...not so fast. Something else you need to plan is your pup's first trip to the veterinarian. Perhaps the breeder can recommend someone in the area who specializes in Newfoundlands, or maybe you know some other owners of large-breed dogs who can suggest a good vet. Either way, you should have an appointment arranged for your pup before you pick him up.

SKULL & CROSSBONES
Thoroughly Newf-proof your house before bringing your puppy home. Never use cockroach or rodent poisons or plant fertilizers in any area accessible to the dog. Avoid the use of toilet cleaners. Most dogs are born with "toilet-bowl sonar" and will take a drink if the lid is left open. Also keep the trash secured and out of reach.

Scour your garage for potential doggie dangers. Remove weed killers, pesticides and antifreeze materials. Antifreeze is highly toxic and just a few drops can kill a puppy or an adult dog. The sweet taste attracts the animal, who will quickly consume it from the floor or pavement.

The pup's first visit will consist of an overall examination to make sure that the pup does not have any problems that are not apparent to you. The veterinarian will also set up a schedule for the pup's vaccinations; the breeder will inform you of which ones the pup has already received and the vet can continue from there.

INTRODUCTION TO THE FAMILY

Everyone in the house will be excited about the puppy's coming home and will want to pet him and play with him, but it is best to make the introductions low-key so as not to overwhelm the puppy. He is apprehensive already. It is the first time he has been separated from his mother and the breeder, and the ride to your home is likely to be the first time he has been in a car. The last thing you want to do is smother him, as this will only frighten him further. This is not to say that human contact is not extremely necessary at this stage, because this is the time when a connection between the pup and his human family is

Who can resist a Newf puppy? Begin training your puppy from the day he arrives at your home. He will depend on you for his education as well as for attention and companionship.

formed. Gentle petting and soothing words should help console him, as well as just putting him down and letting him explore on his own (under your watchful eye, of course).

The pup may approach the family members or may busy himself with exploring for a while. Gradually, each person should spend some time with the pup, one at a time, crouch-

FEEDING TIPS

You will probably start feeding your pup the same food that he has been getting from the breeder; the breeder should give you a few days' supply to start you off. Although you should not give your pup too many treats, you will want to have puppy treats on hand for coaxing, training, rewards, etc. Be careful, though, as you don't want to overdo it. Too many treats can spoil the balance of your Newf's regular food, as well as contribute to obesity.

ing down to get as close to the pup's level as possible and letting him sniff their hands while petting him gently. He definitely needs human attention and he needs to be touched—this is how to form an immediate bond. Just remember that the pup is experiencing a lot of things for the first time, at the same time. There are new people, new noises, new smells and new things to investigate, so be gentle, be affectionate and be as comforting as you can be.

Introducing your Newfie to children should be done with care, keeping in mind that a full-grown Newf easily outweighs most kids! Likewise, children must be taught the proper way to treat a dog.

PUP'S FIRST NIGHT HOME

You have traveled home with your new charge safely in his crate. He's been to the vet for a thorough check-up; he's been weighed, his papers examined;

perhaps he's even been vaccinated and wormed as well. He's met the whole family, including the excited children and the less-than-happy cat. He's explored his area, his new bed, the yard and anywhere else he's been permitted. He's eaten his first meal at home and relieved himself in the proper place. He's heard lots of new sounds, smelled new friends and seen more of the outside world than ever before. That was just the first day! He's worn out

IN DUE TIME

It will take at least two weeks for your puppy to become accustomed to his new surroundings. Give him lots of love, attention, handling, frequent opportunities to relieve himself, a diet he likes to eat and a place he can call his own.

and is ready for bed...or so you think!

It's puppy's first night and you are ready to say "Good night"—keep in mind that this is puppy's first night ever to be sleeping alone. His dam and littermates are no longer at paw's length and he's a bit scared, cold and lonely. Be reassuring to your new family member, but this is not the time to spoil him and give in to his inevitable whining.

Puppies whine. They whine to let others know where they are and hopefully to get company out of it. Place your pup in his new bed or crate in his room and close the door. Mercifully, he may fall asleep without a peep. When the inevitable occurs, ignore the whining: he is fine. Be strong and keep his interest in mind. Do not allow yourself to feel guilty and visit the pup. He will fall asleep eventually.

Many breeders recommend placing a piece of bedding from his former home in his new bed so that he recognizes the scent of his littermates. Others still advise placing a hot water bottle in his bed for warmth. This latter may be a good idea provided the pup doesn't attempt to suckle—he'll get good and wet and may not fall asleep so fast.

Puppy's first night can be somewhat stressful for the pup and his new family. Remember that you are setting the tone of nighttime at your house. Unless you want to play with your pup every night at 10 p.m., midnight and 2 a.m., don't initiate the habit. Your family will thank you, and soon so will your pup!

PREVENTING PUPPY PROBLEMS

SOCIALIZATION

Now that you have done all of the preparatory work and have helped your pup get accustomed to his new home and family, it is about time for you to have some fun! Socializing your Newfoundland pup gives you the opportunity to show off your new friend, and your pup gets to reap the benefits of being an adorable furry creature that people will want to pet and, in general, think is absolutely precious!

Besides getting to know his new family, your puppy should be exposed to other people, animals and situations, but of course he must not come into close contact with dogs you don't know well until his course of injections is fully complete. Socialization will help your Newf become well adjusted as he grows up and less prone to being timid or fearful of the new things he will encounter. Your pup's socialization began with the breeder, but now it is your responsibility to continue it. The socialization he receives up

MANNERS MATTER
During the socialization process, a puppy should meet people, experience different environments and definitely be exposed to other canines. Through playing and interacting with other dogs, your puppy will learn lessons, ranging from controlling the pressure of his jaws by biting his littermates to the inner-workings of the canine pack that he will apply to his human relationships for the rest of his life. That is why removing a puppy from the litter too early (before eight weeks) can be detrimental to the pup's development.

until the age of 12 weeks is the most critical, as this is the time when he forms his impressions of the outside world. Be especially careful during the eight-to-ten-week-old period, also known as the fear period. The interaction he receives during this time should be gentle and reassuring. Lack of socialization or negative socialization experiences can manifest in fear and aggression as the dog grows up. He needs lots of human contact, affection, handling and exposure to other animals.

Once your pup has received his necessary vaccinations, feel free to take him out and about (on his lead, of course). Walk him around the neighborhood, take him on your daily errands, let people pet him, let him meet other dogs and pets, etc. Puppies do not have to try to make friends; there will be no shortage of people who will want to intro-

From the happy roll of this Newf, you can tell that he loves having a place to play outdoors.

> ### PUP MEETS WORLD
> Thorough socialization includes not only meeting new people but also being introduced to new experiences such as riding in the car, having his coat brushed, hearing the television, walking in a crowd—the list is endless. The more your pup experiences, and the more positive the experiences are, the less of a shock and the less frightening it will be for your pup to encounter new things.

duce themselves. Just make sure that you carefully supervise each meeting. If the neighborhood children want to say hello, for example, that is great—children and pups most often make great companions. However, sometimes an excited child can unintentionally handle a pup too roughly, or an overzealous pup can playfully nip a little too hard. You want to make socialization experiences positive ones. What a pup learns during this very formative stage will affect his attitude toward future encounters. You want your dog to be comfortable around everyone. A pup that has a bad experience with a child may grow up to be a dog that is shy around or aggressive toward children.

CONSISTENCY IN TRAINING
Dogs, being pack animals, naturally need a leader, or else they try to establish dominance in

their packs. When you welcome a dog into your family, the choice of who becomes the leader and who becomes the "pack" is entirely up to you! Your pup's intuitive quest for dominance, coupled with the fact that it is nearly impossible to look at an adorable Newfoundland pup with his "puppy-dog" eyes and not cave in, give the pup almost an unfair advantage in getting the upper hand!

A pup will definitely test the waters to see what he can and cannot do. Do not give in to those pleading eyes—stand your ground when it comes to disciplining the pup and make sure that all family members do the same. It will only confuse the pup when Mother tells him to get off the sofa when he is used to sitting up there with Father to watch the nightly news. Avoid discrepancies by having all members of the household decide on the rules before the pup even comes home...and be consistent in enforcing them! Early training shapes the dog's personality, so you cannot be unclear in what you expect.

COMMON PUPPY PROBLEMS

The best way to prevent puppy problems is to be proactive in stopping an undesirable behavior as soon as it starts. The old saying "You can't teach an old dog new tricks" does not neces-

TRAINING TIP

Training your dog takes much patience and can be frustrating at times, but you should see results from your efforts. If you have a Newfie that seems untrainable, take him to a trainer or behaviorist. The dog may have a personality problem that requires the help of a professional, or perhaps you need help in learning how to train your dog.

sarily hold true, but it *is* true that it is much easier to discourage bad behavior in a young developing pup than to wait until the pup's bad behavior becomes the adult dog's bad habit. There are some problems that are especially prevalent in puppies as they develop.

Instill good habits in your Newfie pup, and he should be a mannerly dog throughout his life.

friendly nip, but he also does not know his own strength.

CRYING/WHINING

Your pup will often cry, whine, whimper, howl or make some type of commotion when he is left alone. This is basically his

NIPPING

As puppies start to teethe, they feel the need to sink their teeth into anything available...unfortunately, that includes your fingers, arms, hair and toes. You may find this behavior cute for the first five seconds...until you feel just how sharp those puppy teeth are. This is something you want to discourage immediately and consistently with a firm "No!" (or whatever number of firm "Nos" it takes for him to understand that you mean business). Then replace your finger with an appropriate chew toy. While this behavior is merely annoying when the dog is young, it can become dangerous as your Newfoundland's adult teeth grow in and his jaws develop if he continues to think it is okay to nip and nibble on his human friends. Your Newfoundland does not mean any harm with a

TOXIC TREATS

Treats are helpful motivators in training and welcome rewards for good behavior. However, be careful of "people foods" that are toxic to dogs. For example, chocolate contains the chemical thebromine, which is poisonous to dogs, although "chocolates" especially made for dogs are safe (as they don't actually contain chocolate) but not recommended. Any item that encourages your dog to enjoy the taste of cocoa should be discouraged. You should also exercise caution when using mulch in your garden. This frequently contains cocoa hulls, and dogs have been known to die from eating the mulch. Onions are another food poisonous to dogs.

way of calling out for attention to make sure that you know he is there and that you have not forgotten about him. He feels insecure when he is left alone, when you are out of the house and he is in his crate or when you are in another part of the house and he cannot see you. The noise he is making is an expression of the anxiety he feels at being alone, so he needs to be taught that being alone is okay. You are not actually training the dog to stop making noise, you are training him to feel comfortable when he is alone and thus removing the need for him to make the noise.

This is where the crate with cozy bedding and a toy comes in handy. You want to know that he is safe when you are not there to supervise, and you know that he will be safe in his crate rather

than roaming freely about the house. In order for the pup to stay in his crate without making a fuss, he needs to be comfortable in his crate. On that note, it is extremely important that the crate is never used as a form of punishment, or the pup will develop a negative association with the crate.

Accustom the pup to the crate in short, gradually increasing time intervals in which you put him in the crate, maybe with a treat, and stay in the room with him. If he cries or makes a fuss, do not go to him, but stay in his sight. Gradually he will realize that staying in his crate is just fine without your help, and it will not be so traumatic for him when you are not around. You may want to leave the radio on softly when you leave the house; the sound of human voices may be comforting to him.

The sweet and gentle Newfoundland is a lovable, kissable character.

PUPPY PROBLEMS

The majority of problems that are commonly seen in young pups will disappear as your dog gets older. However, how you deal with problems when he is young will determine how he reacts to discipline as an adult dog. It is important to establish who is boss (ideally it will be you!) right away when you are first bonding with your dog. This bond will set the tone for the rest of your life together.

FEEDING YOUR NEWFIE

Feeding a dog that will grow from about 1 lb at birth to 100–150 lb in one year presents more challenge than feeding a medium- or average-sized dog. There is a natural human tendency to feed "more" so the dog can grow bigger, faster. That is a recipe for skeletal disaster, as a puppy's joints are extremely vulnerable during this period of rapid growth, and over-nutrition can easily stress his growing bones.

That said, the Newf puppy does require a large amount of good-quality food to support such rapid growth. He should receive four small meals a day during his first twelve weeks, reducing the frequency to three meals a day until six months of age. Thereafter the pup should eat twice daily for his entire lifetime. Do not offer table scraps or supplements of any kind, nor should your puppy be given supplemental vitamins or extra calcium. A top-quality food is perfectly formulated and balanced to provide proper nutrition to support healthy growth and maintenance. Supplements and additives will upset that delicate balance and may cause serious growth and skeletal problems in a pup.

It is most important that you not allow a Newf puppy to get fat. The excess weight will stress his growing joints, increase the possibility of future health problems and decrease his life expectancy. It is best to consult the breeder for advice about a healthy and balanced nutrition program.

Today the choices of food for your Newfoundland are many and varied. There are simply dozens of brands of food in all sorts of flavors and textures, ranging from

GRAIN-BASED DIETS

Some less expensive dog foods are based on grains and other plant proteins. While these products may appear to be attractively priced, many breeders prefer a diet based on animal proteins and believe that they are more conducive to your dog's health. Many grain-based diets rely on soy protein, which may cause flatulence (passing gas).

There are many cases, however, when your dog might require a special diet. These special requirements should only be recommended by your veterinarian.

puppy diets to those for seniors. There are even hypoallergenic and low-calorie diets available. Because your Newfoundland's food has a bearing on coat, health and temperament, it is essential that the most suitable diet is selected for a Newfoundland of his age. It is fair to say, however, that even experienced owners can be perplexed by the enormous range of foods available. Only understanding what is best for your dog will help you reach an informed decision.

Dog foods are produced in three basic types: dry, semi-moist and canned. Dry foods are useful for the cost-conscious, for overall they tend to be less expensive than semi-moist or canned. They also contain the least fat and the most preservatives. In general, canned foods are made up of 60–70% water, while semi-moist ones often contain so much sugar that they are perhaps the least preferred by owners, even though their dogs seem to like them.

When selecting your dog's diet, three stages of development must be considered: the puppy stage, the adult stage and the senior stage.

PUPPY STAGE

Puppies instinctively want to suck milk from their mother's teats, and a normal puppy will exhibit this behavior from just a few moments following birth. If

---

FEEDING TIPS

- Dog food must be served at room temperature, neither too hot nor too cold. Fresh water, changed often and served in a clean bowl, is mandatory.
- Never feed your dog from the table while you are eating, and never feed your dog leftovers from your own meal. They usually contain too much fat and too much seasoning.
- Dogs must chew their food. Hard pellets are excellent; soups and stews are to be avoided.
- Don't add leftovers or any extras to commercial dog food. The normal food is usually balanced, and adding something extra destroys the balance.
- Except for age-related changes, dogs do not require dietary variations. They can be fed the same diet, day after day, without their becoming bored or ill.

"DOES THIS COLLAR MAKE ME LOOK FAT?"

Obesity is the number-one health problem in 21st-century canines. The excessive weight will stress the dog's joints and vital organs and can lead to a premature death. While humans may obsess about how they look and how trim their bodies are, many people believe that extra weight on their dogs is a good thing. The truth is, pets should not be over- or underweight, as both can lead to or signal sickness. In order to tell how fit your pet is, run your hands over his ribs. Are his ribs buried under a layer of fat or are they sticking out considerably? If your pet is within his normal weight range, you should be able to feel the ribs easily. If you stand above him, the outline of his body should resemble an hourglass. Some breeds do tend to be leaner while some are a bit stockier, but making sure your dog is the right weight for his breed will certainly contribute to his good health.

puppies do not attempt to suckle within the first half-hour or so, they should be encouraged to do so by placing them on the nipples, having selected ones with plenty of milk. This early milk supply is important in providing colostrum to protect the puppies during the first eight to ten weeks of their lives. Although a mother's milk is much better than any milk formula, despite there being some excellent ones available, if the puppies do not feed, the breeder will have to feed them himself. For those with less experience, advice from a veterinarian is important so that not only the right quantity of milk is fed but also that of correct quality, fed at suitably frequent intervals, usually every two hours during the first few days of life.

Puppies should be allowed to nurse from their mothers for about the first six weeks, although from the third or fourth week the breeder will begin to introduce small portions of suitable solid food. Most breeders like to introduce alternate milk and meat meals initially, building up to weaning time.

By the time the puppies are seven or a maximum of eight weeks old, they should be fully weaned and fed solely on a complete food. Selection of the most suitable, good-quality diet at this time is essential, for a Newf puppy's fastest growth rate is during the first 18 months of life. Your vet and breeder will be able to offer advice in this regard. During his growth period between 3 and 18 months, he will eat more (proportionately to size) than he will as an adult.

As discussed, the frequency of meals will be reduced over time. Puppy and junior diets should be well balanced for the needs of your dog, so that except in certain circumstances advised by the vet, additional vitamins, minerals and proteins will not be required.

ADULT DIETS

A dog generally is considered an adult when he has stopped growing; in the Newf, this is around 18 months of age. Again you should rely upon your veterinarian or breeder to recommend an acceptable maintenance diet. An adult Newf is a comparatively small eater for his size. Amounts to feed are based on the individual dog's size and activity. Major dog-food manufacturers specialize in this type of food, and it is merely necessary for you to select the one best suited to your dog's needs. Active dogs have different requirements than more sedate dogs.

SENIOR DIETS

As dogs get older, their metabolism changes. The older dog usually exercises less, moves more slowly and sleeps more. This change in lifestyle and phys-

iological performance requires a change in diet. Since these changes take place slowly, they might not be recognizable. What

TIPPING THE SCALES

Good nutrition is vital to your dog's health, but many people end up over-feeding or giving unnecessary supplements. Here are some common doggie diet don'ts:

- Adding milk, yogurt and cheese to your dog's diet may seem like a good idea for coat and skin care, but dairy products are very fattening and can cause indigestion.
- Diets high in fat will not cause heart attacks in dogs but will certainly cause your dog to gain weight.
- Most importantly, don't assume your dog will simply stop eating once he doesn't need any more food. Given the chance, he will eat you out of house and home!

Newfs have lifespans of about eight to ten years, most experts would consider a Newf a senior at six or seven years, which proves a suitable time to begin offering a senior diet.

WATER

Just as your dog needs proper nutrition from his food, water is an essential "nutrient" as well.

Not much is out of your Newf's reach when it comes to snatching a snack! Sweets are not good for dogs and can lead to an upset stomach or worse.

is easily recognizable is weight gain. By continuing to feed your dog an adult-maintenance diet when he is slowing down meta-bolically, your dog will gain weight. Obesity in an older dog compounds the health problems that already accompany old age.

As your dog gets older, few of his organs function up to par. The kidneys slow down and the intestines become less efficient. These age-related factors are best handled with a change in diet and a change in feeding schedule to give smaller portions that are more easily digested.

There is no single best diet for every older dog. While many dogs do well on light or senior diets, other dogs do better on puppy diets or special premium diets such as lamb and rice. Be sensitive to your senior Newfoundland's diet and this will help control other problems that may arise with your old friend. Since

CHANGE IN DIET

As your dog's caretaker, you know the importance of keeping his diet consistent, but sometimes when you run out of food or if you're on vacation, you have to make a change quickly. Some dogs will experience digestive problems, but most will not. If you are planning on changing your dog's menu, do so gradually to ensure that your dog will not have any problems. Over a period of four to five days, slowly add some new food to your dog's old food, increasing the percentage of new food each day.

A Worthy Investment

Veterinary studies have proven that a balanced high-quality diet pays off in your dog's coat quality, behavior and activity level. Invest in premium brands for the maximum payoff with your dog.

frisky. Because the Newf is people-oriented and has a strong desire to please his owner, he is easily motivated to activity if his owner is involved.

Rough-house games are never recommended for Newfie puppies or adults. The breed's teddy-bear appearance makes it very tempting to wrestle or play tug-of-war. However, those same games will not be fun when the Newf has grown from a 25-lb puppy to a 150-lb adult and throws body

Swimming is wonderful exercise for the Newfoundland. It puts no impact on the dog's bones and joints while providing activity that comes naturally to this seafaring breed.

Water keeps the dog's body properly hydrated and promotes normal function of the body's systems. During housebreaking, it is necessary to keep an eye on how much water your Newfoundland is drinking, but, once he is reliably trained, he should have free access to clean fresh water at all times. Make certain that the dog's water bowl is clean and elevated, and change the water often.

EXERCISE

The adult Newfoundland requires a session or two of brisk daily exercise with his owner. He will not be motivated to exercise alone; you are his incentive to walk, trot and play. Adult Newfs have a fairly low metabolism and thus tend to become lazy "couch potatoes" unless stimulated to move about or get

DRINK, DRANK, DRUNK—MAKE IT A DOUBLE

In both humans and dogs, as well as other living organisms, water forms the major part of nearly every body tissue. Naturally, we take water for granted, but without it, life as we know it would cease.

For dogs, water is needed to keep their bodies functioning biochemically. Additionally, water is needed to replace the water lost while panting. Unlike humans, who are able to sweat to dissipate heat, dogs must pant to cool down, thereby losing the vital water that their bodies need to regulate their body temperatures. Humans lose electrolyte-containing products and other body-fluid components through sweating; dogs do not lose anything except water.

Water is essential always, but especially so when the weather is hot or humid or when your dog is exercising or working vigorously.

Although the Newf has lazy tendencies, he will surely spring to action for some playtime with his owner.

blocks that knock you or your neighbors to the ground.

Such rough-and-tumble tactics are also dangerous for a fast-growing breed whose joints are very vulnerable during their rapid-growth stage. Over-exercise is unhealthy for immature joints and can lead to serious orthopedic problems in a growing pup. Newf pups should be introduced to gentle play games, creating healthy habits that they will carry with them all through life.

Outdoor walks are still the best exercise for a Newf of any age. He will also enjoy lively games of "fetch," which will tweak his natural retrieving instincts as well as teach him the basic obedience command to

return to you when called. Most breeders will be happy to suggest enjoyable and healthy exercise regimens for their Newf puppies for youth and into adulthood.

GROOMING

Grooming is essential to the overall health of a heavy-coated breed like the Newfoundland. A thorough brushing at least once a week will keep his coat in good condition and help reduce body odor and the incidence of bacterial skin infections. Newfs shed their coats most heavily in the spring, "blowing" their thick undercoats in huge quantities. They shed once again in fall, although this is not as mind-boggling as in spring. More

A Newfie's coat requires regular attention. Daily brushing is ideal and saves time in the long run, keeping the coat tangle-free.

more easily and require frequent attention to avoid serious clumping as the old hair loosens and falls out. One must take special care to tidy up around and behind the ears, inside and behind the hind legs, under the chest and the tail, and all the feathering as well. If you introduce your Newfie to grooming early in life, he will look forward to his grooming sessions and the personal one-on-one attention. Otherwise, grooming sessions become more like wrestling matches between the Newf and owner, a ticklish situa-

LET THE SUN SHINE

Your dog needs daily sunshine for the same reason people do. Pets kept inside homes with curtains drawn against the sun suffer from "SAD" (Seasonal Affected Disorder) to the same degree as humans. We now know that sunlight must enter the iris and thus progress to the pineal gland to regulate the body's hormonal system. When we live and work in artificial light, both circadian rhythms and hormone balances are disturbed.

Spend a few minutes each day brushing your pup with a slicker brush to accustom him to grooming.

frequent grooming sessions are requisite during those shedding periods to collect the vast amounts of hair dispatched by the dog. It is important to brush out the dead coat or mats will form, making future grooming difficult and even painful. The dead hair also provides nasty host sites for bacterial infections under the matted coat.

Because of the Newfie's dense, heavy coat, areas around the ears, legs, chest and tail develop mats

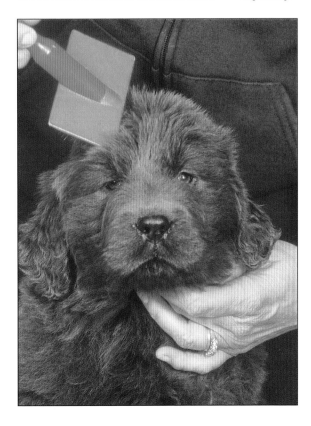

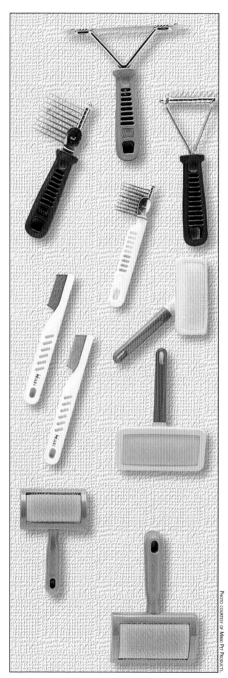

Purchase top-quality grooming tools to keep your Newfie's coat in good condition and to last through frequent use.

tion since the dog often outweighs his human.

Proper grooming tools are a wise investment for every Newfie owner. They make the task less of a chore and will help keep the dog looking neat and tidy. Check with the breeder about the tools that he prefers. The most commonly used implements include thinning shears, blunt-tip scissors, a long-tooth steel comb, a slicker brush, a mat/tangle rake, dental-care items and a nail clipper. Quality tools are easier to use, last longer and produce a better looking end result.

Most Newfoundlands do not require frequent bathing; four times a year is sufficient for dogs that are groomed on a regular

GROOMING EQUIPMENT

Always purchase the best quality grooming equipment so that your tools will last for many years to come. Here are some basics:

- Slicker brush
- Metal comb
- Grooming rake
- Blunt-tip scissors
- Thinning shears
- Rubber mat
- Dog shampoo
- Towels
- Blow dryer
- Ear cleaner
- Cotton balls
- Nail clippers
- Dental-care products

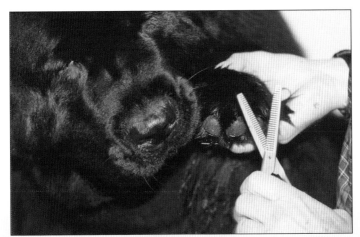

Thinning shears may be used to tidy up the hairs around the dog's feet.

Hair around the ears may also be trimmed with the thinning shears.

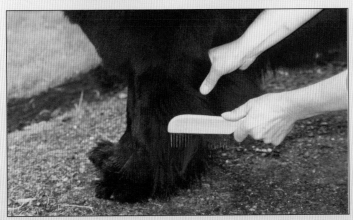

Metal combs are used for removing tangles and keeping the coat free of foreign matter.

Professional groomers as well as serious exhibitors usually have grooming tables on which to stand their dogs. Investing in a grooming table now may save you money at the chiropractor's office later on. Grooming a Newf is not very easy on the back!

DRYING OUT
A freshly bathed Newfoundland coat can take as long as 24 hours to dry.

basis. A dog that is shown in conformation may need bathing a bit more often. Frequency depends on the owner's fussiness and the lifestyle of the dog. Farm-raised dogs that love to roll around in not-so-pleasant areas will surely require more frequent baths.

BATHING

Dogs do not need to be bathed as often as humans, but bathing as needed is essential for healthy skin and a clean, shiny coat. Again, like most anything, if you accustom your pup to being bathed as a puppy, it will be second nature by the time he grows up. You want your dog to be at ease in the bath or else it could end up a wet, soapy, messy ordeal for both of you!

Brush your Newfoundland thoroughly before wetting his coat. A rake is especially helpful during times of shedding. This will get rid of most mats and tangles, which are harder to remove when the coat is wet. Make certain that your dog has a good non-slip surface to stand on. Begin by wetting the dog's coat. A shower or hose attachment is necessary for thoroughly wetting and rinsing the coat. Check the water temperature to make sure that it is neither too hot nor too cold for the dog.

Next, apply shampoo to the dog's coat and work it into a good lather. You should purchase a shampoo that is made for dogs. Do not use a product made for human hair, as these are too strong and will strip the dog's coat of essential oils needed to keep the coat water-resistant. Wash the head

Feeding the right foods to keep teeth clean and making tooth-brushing part of your grooming routine will prevent tooth and gum disease and add to your Newf's life.

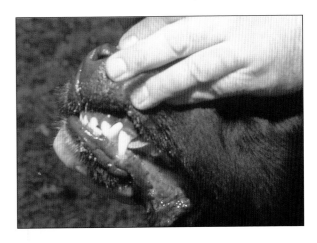

PEDICURE TIP

A dog that spends a lot of time outside on a hard surface, such as cement or pavement, will have his nails naturally worn down and may not need to have them trimmed as often, except maybe in the colder months when he is not outside as much. Regardless, it is best to get your dog accustomed to the nail-trimming procedure at an early age so that he is used to it. Some dogs are especially sensitive about having their feet touched, but if a dog has experienced it since puppyhood, it should not bother him.

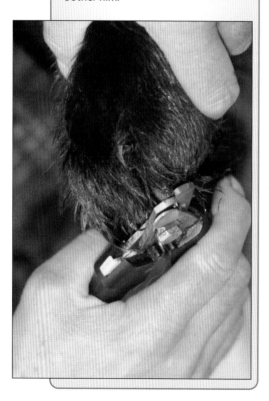

last; you do not want shampoo to drip into the dog's eyes while you are washing the rest of his body. Work the shampoo all the way down to the skin. You can use this opportunity to check the skin for any bumps, bites or other abnormalities. Do not neglect any area of the body—get all of the hard-to-reach places.

Once the dog has been thoroughly shampooed, he requires an equally thorough rinsing. Shampoo left in the coat can be irritating to the skin. Protect his eyes from the shampoo by shielding them with your hand and directing the flow of water in the opposite direction. You should also avoid getting water in the ear canal. Be prepared for your dog to shake out his coat—you might want to stand back, but make sure you have a hold on the dog to keep him from running through the house. Have a heavy towel ready, and you may choose to finish drying with a blow-dryer on a low heat setting or just letting the coat finish drying naturally.

EAR CLEANING

The ears should be kept clean with a cotton ball and ear powder or liquid made especially for dogs. Be on the lookout for any signs of infection or ear-mite infestation. If your Newfoundland has been shaking his head or scratching at his ears frequently, this usually indicates a problem. If his ears

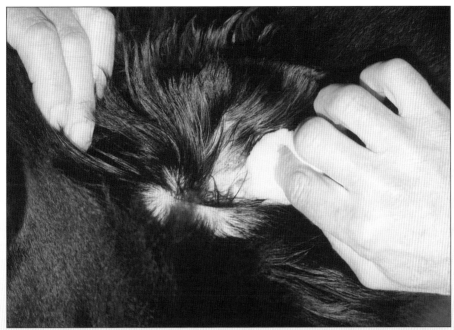

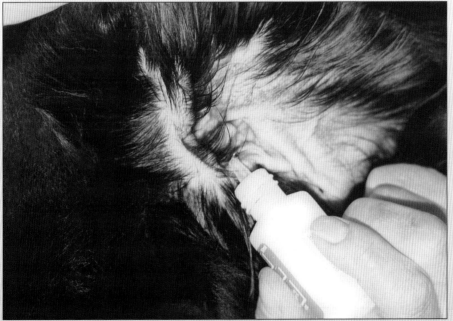

Your Newfie's ears should be cleaned on a regular basis, using an ear-cleaning product formulated for dogs and soft cotton, both of which are usually available at your pet shop.

Nail Maintenance

Nail Casing

Quick

Cut Line

Dark-Colored Nails

With black or dark nails, where the quick is not easy to see, it's best to clip only the tip of the nail or to use a file.

Light-Colored Nails

In light-colored nails, clipping is much simpler because you can see the vein (or quick) that grows inside the casing.

have an unusual odor, this is a sure sign of mite infestation or infection, and a signal to have his ears checked by the veterinarian.

NAIL CLIPPING

Nail clipping is also an important part of a Newf's grooming agenda. Short nails prevent the feet from splaying, which is a common problem in giant breeds. Your Newfoundland should be accustomed to having his nails trimmed at an early age, since it will be part of your maintenance routine throughout his life. Not only do short nails look nicer, but long nails can scratch someone unintentionally. Also, a long nail has a better chance of ripping and bleeding, or causing the feet to spread. A good rule of thumb is that if you can hear your dog's nails' clicking on the floor when he walks, his nails are too long.

Before you start cutting, make sure you can identify the "quick" in each nail. The quick is a blood vessel that runs through the center of each nail and grows rather close to the end. It will bleed if accidentally cut, which will be quite painful for the dog as it contains nerve endings. Keep some type of clotting agent on hand, such as a styptic pencil or styptic powder (the type used for shaving). This will stop the bleeding quickly when applied to the end of the cut nail. Do not panic if you cut the quick, just stop the bleeding and

TRAVEL ALERT

Never leave your dog alone in the car. In hot weather, your dog can die from the high temperature inside a closed vehicle; even a car parked in the shade can heat up very quickly. Leaving the window open is dangerous as well since the dog can hurt himself trying to get out.

talk soothingly to your dog. Once he has calmed down, move on to the next nail. It is better to clip a little at a time, particularly with dark-nailed dogs.

Hold your pup steady as you begin trimming his nails; you do not want him to make any sudden movements or run away. Talk to him soothingly and stroke him as you clip. Holding his foot in your hand, simply take off the end of each nail in one quick clip. You can purchase nail clippers that are specially made for dogs; you can probably find them wherever you buy pet supplies.

TRAVELING WITH YOUR DOG

CAR TRAVEL

You should accustom your Newfoundland to riding in a car at an early age. You may or may not take him in the car often, but at the very least he will need to go

Because of their size, crates suitable for adult Newfies are inconvenient to load and unload. Investigate safety dividers to keep your Newf safe when traveling by car.

EXERCISE CAUTION

You should be careful where you exercise your dog. Many areas have been sprayed with chemicals that are highly toxic to both dogs and humans. Never allow your dog to eat grass or drink from puddles on either public or private grounds, as the run-off water may contain chemicals from sprays and herbicides.

the vehicle and away from the driver. Another option is a specially made safety harness for dogs, which straps the dog in much like a seat belt. Do not let the dog roam loose in the vehicle—this is very dangerous! If you should stop short, your dog can be thrown and injured. If the dog starts climbing on you and pestering you while you are driving, you will not be able to concentrate on the road. It is an unsafe situation for everyone—human and canine.

For long trips, bring along water to offer to your dog and be prepared to make stops to let the dog relieve himself. Take with you whatever you need to clean up after him, including some paper towels and perhaps some old rags for use should he have an accident in the car or suffer from motion sickness.

AIR TRAVEL

Contact your chosen airline before proceeding with travel plans that include your Newfoundland. The dog will be required to travel in a fiberglass crate and you should always check in advance with the airline regarding specific requirements for the crate's size, type and labeling, as well as any travel restrictions (such as during the summer months) and health certificates needed for the dog.

To help put your Newfoundland at ease for the trip, be sure he is well acclimated to the crate

to the vet and you do not want these trips to be traumatic for the dog or troublesome for you. The safest way for a puppy to ride in the car is in his crate. If he uses a crate in the house, you can use the same crate for travel, or you can get a smaller travel crate for the pup. As your Newf grows up, it may not be feasible to take him along in a crate, unless you have a vehicle that is large enough to accommodate a giant crate.

A safety gate can also serve to keep the Newf in the rear part of

in which he will be traveling and give him one of his favorite toys in the crate. Do not feed the dog for several hours prior to checking in so that you minimize his need to relieve himself. Some airlines require you to provide documentation as to when the dog was last fed. In any case, a light meal is best. For long trips, you will have to attach food and water bowls and a portion of food to the outside of the dog's crate so that airline employees can tend to him between legs of the trip.

Make sure that your dog is properly identified and that your contact information appears on his ID tags and on his crate. Your Newfoundland will travel in a different area of the plane than the human passengers, so every rule must be strictly followed to prevent any risk of getting separated from your dog.

VACATIONS AND BOARDING

So you want to take a family vacaion—and you want to include *all* members of the family. You would probably make arrangements for accommodations ahead of time anyway, but this is especially important when traveling with a dog (even more so with a large dog). You do not want to make an overnight stop at the only place around for miles and find out that they do not allow dogs. Also, you do not want to reserve a place for your family without confirming that you are traveling with a dog because, if it is against their policy, you may end up without a place to stay.

Alternatively, if you are traveling and choose not to bring your Newfoundland, you will have to make arrangements for him while you are away. Some options are to take him to a friends's house to stay while you are gone, to have a

Traveling with a Newf requires a *big* vehicle and attention to your dog's comfort and safety.

ON-LEAD ONLY

When traveling, never let your dog off-lead in a strange area. Your dog could run away out of fear, decide to chase a passing squirrel or cat or simply want to stretch his legs without restriction—if any of these happen, you might never see your canine friend again.

It is recommended that you research boarding kennels near your home before you actually need to use one. You will need to find a facility that affords your Newf ample space and attention.

IDENTITY CRISIS!

Surely you know the importance of good nutrition, good training and a good home, but are you aware of the importance of identification tags for your dog? If your dog ran away or got lost, ID tags on your pet's collar would provide crucial information such as the dog's name and your name and contact information, making it possible that your dog would soon be returned. Every morning before taking your dog out, make sure his collar and tags are present and securely fastened.

trusted neighbor stop by often or stay at your house or to bring your dog to a reputable boarding kennel. If you choose to board him at a kennel, you should visit in advance to see the facilities provided, how clean they are and where the dogs are kept. Talk to some of the employees and see how they treat the dogs—do they spend time with the dogs, play with them, exercise them, etc.? Does the kennel have ample space for your giant friend? Also find out the kennel's policy on vaccinations and what they require. This is for all of the dogs' safety,

since when dogs are kept together, there is a greater risk of diseases being passed from dog to dog.

IDENTIFICATION

Your Newfoundland is your valued companion and friend. That is why you always keep a close eye on him and you have made sure that he cannot escape from the yard or wriggle out of his collar and run away from you. However, accidents can happen and there may come a time when your dog unexpectedly gets separated from you. If this unfortunate event should occur, the first thing on your mind will be finding him. Proper identification, including an ID tag, and possibly a tattoo and/or a microchip, will increase the chances of his being returned to you safely and quickly.

IDENTIFICATION OPTIONS

As puppies become more and more expensive, especially those puppies of high quality for showing and/or breeding, they have a greater chance of being stolen. The usual collar dog tag is, of course, easily removed. But there are two more permanent techniques that have become widely used for identifying dogs.

The puppy microchip implantation involves the injection of a small microchip, about the size of a corn kernel, under the skin of the dog. If your dog shows up at a clinic or shelter, or is offered for resale under less-than-savory circumstances, he can be positively identified by the microchip. The microchip is scanned, and a registry quickly identifies you as the owner.

Tattooing is done on various parts of the dog, from his belly to his ears. The number tattooed can be your telephone number, your dog's registration number or any other number that you can easily memorize. When professional dog thieves see a tattooed dog, they usually lose interest. For the safety of our dogs, no laboratory facility or dog broker will accept a tattooed dog as stock.

Discuss microchipping and tattooing with your veterinarian and breeder. Some vets perform these services on their own premises for a reasonable fee. To ensure that your dog's identification is effective, be certain that the dog is then properly registered with a legitimate national database.

Your Newfie should never be without a suitable identification tag attached to a sturdy collar.

TRAINING YOUR

NEWFOUNDLAND

Living with an untrained dog is a lot like owning a piano that you do not know how to play—it is a nice object to look at, but it does not do much more than that to bring you pleasure. Now try taking piano lessons, and suddenly the piano comes alive and brings forth magical sounds and rhythms that set your heart singing and your body swaying.

The same is true with your Newfoundland. Any dog is a big responsibility and, if not trained sensibly, may develop unacceptable behavior that annoys you or could even cause family friction.

To train your Newfoundland, you may like to enroll in an obedience class. Teach him good manners as you learn how and why he behaves the way he does. Find out how to communicate with your dog and how to recognize and understand his communications with you. Suddenly the dog takes on a new role in your life—he is clever, interesting, well-behaved and fun to be with. He demonstrates his bond of devotion to you daily. In other words, your Newfoundland does wonders for your ego because he constantly reminds you that you are not only his leader, you are his hero!

Those involved with teaching dog obedience and counseling owners about their dogs' behavior have discovered some interesting facts about dog ownership. For example, training dogs when they are puppies results in the

PARENTAL GUIDANCE
Training a dog is a life experience. Many parents admit that much of what they know about raising children they learned from caring for their dogs. Dogs respond to love, fairness and guidance, just as children do. Become a good dog owner and you may become an even better parent.

highest rate of success in developing well-mannered and well-adjusted adult dogs. Training an older dog, from six months to six years of age, can produce almost equal results, providing that the owner accepts the dog's slower rate of learning capability and is willing to work patiently to help the dog succeed at developing to his fullest potential. Unfortunately, many owners of untrained adult dogs lack the patience factor, so they do not persist until their dogs are successful at learning particular behaviors.

Training a puppy aged 10 to 16 weeks (20 weeks at the most) is like working with a dry sponge in a pool of water. The pup soaks up whatever you show him and constantly looks for more things to do and learn. At this early age, his body is not yet producing hormones, and therein lies the reason for such a high rate of success. Without hormones, he is focused on his

Begin training your Newf while he is still in the "sponge" stage: ready to soak up every ounce of lesson you can pour on him. Make an effort early on to teach him the basic commands and the rules of the house.

REAP THE REWARDS

If you start with a normal, healthy dog and give him time, patience and some carefully executed lessons, you will reap the rewards of that training for the life of the dog. And what a life it will be! The two of you will find immeasurable pleasure in the companionship you have built together with love, respect and understanding.

owners and not particularly interested in investigating other places, dogs, people, etc. You are his leader: his provider of food, water, shelter and security. He latches onto you and wants to stay close. He will usually follow you from room to room, will not let you out of his sight when you are outdoors with him and will respond in like manner to the people and animals you encounter. If you greet a friend

Keep training sessions enjoyable for the Newfoundland. Convince your Newf that training time means sharing quality time together. This Newf is fairly exploding with enthusiasm for his lesson.

warmly, he will be happy to greet the person as well. If, however, you are hesitant or anxious about the approach of a stranger, he will respond accordingly to you.

Once the puppy begins to produce hormones, his natural curiosity emerges and he begins to investigate the world around him. It is at this time when you may notice that the untrained dog begins to wander away from you and even ignore your commands to stay close. When this behavior becomes a problem, the owner has two choices: get rid of the dog or train him. It is strongly urged that you choose the latter option.

There usually will be classes within a reasonable distance from your home, but you can also do a lot to train your dog yourself. Sometimes there are classes available, but the tuition is too costly. Whatever the circumstances, the solution to training your Newf without formal obedience lessons lies within the pages of this book.

This chapter is devoted to helping you train your Newfoundland at home. If the recommended procedures are followed faithfully, you may expect positive results that will prove rewarding both to you and your dog.

Whether your new charge is a puppy or a mature adult, the methods of teaching and the

THINK BEFORE YOU BARK
Dogs are sensitive to their masters' moods and emotions. Use your voice wisely when communicating with your dog. Never raise your voice at your dog unless you are trying to correct him. "Barking" at your dog can become as meaningless as "dogspeak" is to you.

techniques we use in training basic behaviors are the same. After all, no dog, whether puppy or adult, likes harsh or inhumane methods. All creatures, however, respond favorably to gentle motivational methods and sincere praise and encouragement. Now let us get started.

HOUSE-TRAINING
You can train your puppy to relieve himself wherever you choose, but this must be somewhere suitable. You should bear in mind from the outset that when your puppy is old enough

HOW MANY TIMES A DAY?

AGE	RELIEF TRIPS
To 14 weeks	10
14–22 weeks	8
22–32 weeks	6
Adulthood	4
(dog stops growing)	

These are estimates, of course, but they are a guide to the *minimum* number of opportunities a dog should have each day to relieve himself.

to go out in public places, any canine deposits must be removed at once. You will always have to carry with you a small plastic bag or "poop-scoop."

Outdoor training includes such surfaces as grass, soil and cement. Indoor training usually means training your dog to newspaper, not a good option with a dog the size of the Newf. When deciding on the surface and location that you will want your

Newfoundland to use, be sure it is going to be permanent. Training your dog to grass and then changing your mind two months later is extremely difficult for both dog and owner.

Next, choose the command you will use each and every time you want your puppy to void. "Hurry up" and "Potty" are examples of commands commonly used by dog owners. Get in the habit of giving the puppy your chosen relief command before you take him out. That way, when he becomes an adult, you will be able to determine if he wants to go out when you ask him. A confirmation will be signs of interest like wagging his tail, watching you intently, going to the door, etc.

PUPPY'S NEEDS

Puppy needs to relieve himself after play periods, after each meal, after he has been sleeping and at any time he indicates that he is looking for a place to urinate or defecate. The urinary and intestinal tract muscles of very young puppies are not fully developed. Therefore, like human babies, puppies need to relieve themselves frequently.

Take your puppy out often—every hour for an eight-week-old, for example, and always immediately after sleeping and eating. The older the puppy, the less often he will need to relieve himself. Finally, as a mature healthy adult, he will require only three to five relief trips per day.

HOUSING

Since the types of housing and control you provide for your puppy have a direct relationship on the success of house-training, we consider the various aspects of both before we begin training.

Taking a new puppy home and turning him loose in your house can be compared to turning a child loose in a sports arena and telling the child that the place is all his! The sheer enormity of the place would be too much for him to handle.

Instead, offer the puppy clearly defined areas where he can play, sleep, eat and live. A room of the house where the family gathers is the most obvious choice. Puppies are social animals and need to feel a part of the pack right from the start. Hearing your voice, watching

A fenced yard is an ideal situation for house-training your Newf.

you while you are doing things and smelling you nearby are all positive reinforcers that he is now a member of your pack. Usually a family room, the kitchen or a nearby adjoining breakfast area is ideal for providing safety and security for both puppy and owner.

Within that room, there should be a smaller area that the puppy can call his own. An alcove, a wire or fiberglass dog crate or a gated corner from which he can view the activities of his new family will be fine. The size of the area or crate is the key factor here. The area must be large enough for the puppy to lie down and stretch out as well as stand up without rubbing his head on the top, yet small enough so that he cannot relieve himself at one end and

MEALTIME

Mealtime should be a peaceful time for your puppy. Do not put his food and water bowls in a high-traffic area in the house. For example, give him his own little corner of the kitchen where he can eat undisturbed and where he will not be underfoot. Do not allow small children or other family members to disturb the pup when he is eating.

Waiting by the door! Once he's learned the routine, your Newf will let you know when it's time to go out...and come back in!

pup's water intake during house-training so you'll be able to predict when he will need to go out.

CONTROL

By control, we mean helping the puppy to create a lifestyle pattern that will be compatible to that of his human pack (*you*). Just as we guide little children to learn our way of life, we must show the puppy when it is time to play, eat, sleep, exercise and even entertain himself.

Your puppy should always sleep in his crate. He should also learn that, during times of household confusion and excessive human activity such as at breakfast when family members are preparing for the day, he can play by himself in relative safety and comfort in his designated area. Each time you leave the puppy alone, he should under-

sleep at the other without coming into contact with his droppings. Dogs are, by nature, clean animals and will not remain close to their relief areas unless forced to do so. In those cases, they then become dirty dogs and usually remain that way for life.

The designated area should contain clean bedding and a toy. Water must always be available, in a non-spill container, although you'll want to monitor your

PAPER CAPER

Never line your pup's sleeping area with newspaper. Puppy litters are usually raised on newspaper and, once in your home, the puppy will immediately associate newspaper with voiding. Never put newspaper on any floor while house-training, as this will only confuse the puppy. Finally, restrict water intake after evening meals. Offer a few licks at a time—never let a Newf of any age gulp water after meals.

CANINE DEVELOPMENT SCHEDULE

It is important to understand how and at what age a puppy develops into adulthood. If you are a puppy owner, consult the following Canine Development Schedule to determine the stage of development your puppy is currently experiencing. This knowledge will help you as you work with the puppy in the weeks and months ahead.

Period	Age	Characteristics
First to Third	**Birth to Seven Weeks**	Puppy needs food, sleep and warmth, and responds to simple and gentle touching. Needs mother for security and disciplining. Needs littermates for learning and interacting with other dogs. Pup learns to function within a pack and learns pack order of dominance. Begin socializing pup with adults and children for short periods. Pup begins to become aware of his environment.
Fourth	**Eight to Twelve Weeks**	Brain is fully developed. Pup needs socializing with outside world. Remove from mother and littermates. Needs to change from canine pack to human pack. Human dominance necessary. Fear period occurs between 8 and 12 weeks. Avoid fright and pain.
Fifth	**Thirteen to Sixteen Weeks**	Training and formal obedience should begin. Less association with other dogs, more with people, places, situations. Period will pass easily if you remember this is pup's change-to-adolescence time. Be firm and fair. Flight instinct prominent. Permissiveness and over-disciplining can do permanent damage. Praise for good behavior.
Juvenile	**Four to Eight Months**	Another fear period about 7 to 8 months of age. It passes quickly, but be cautious of fright and pain. Sexual maturity reached. Dominant traits established. Dog should understand sit, down, come and stay by now.

Note: These are approximate time frames. Allow for individual differences in puppies.

stand exactly where he is to stay. Puppies are chewers. They cannot tell the difference between things like lamp cords, television wires, shoes, table legs, etc. Chewing into a television wire, for example, can be fatal to the puppy, while a shorted wire can start a fire in the house.

TAKE THE LEAD

Do not carry your dog to his relief area. Lead him there on a leash or, better yet, encourage him to follow you to the spot. If you start carrying him to his spot, you might end up doing this routine forever and your dog will have the satisfaction of having trained *you*.

If the puppy chews on the arm of the chair when he is alone, you will probably discipline him angrily when you get home. Thus, he makes the association that your coming home means he is going to be punished. (He will not remember chewing the chair and is incapable of making the association of the discipline with his naughty deed.) Crating the puppy avoids his engaging in dangerous and destructive behaviors, keeping him safe and out of trouble when you cannot supervise.

Other times of excitement, such as family parties, etc., can be fun for the puppy, providing he can view the activities from the security of his designated area. He is not underfoot and he is not being fed all sorts of tidbits that will probably cause him stomach distress, yet he still feels a part of the fun.

SCHEDULE

A puppy should be taken to his relief area each time he is released from his designated area, after meals, after play sessions and when he first awakens in the morning (at age eight weeks, this can mean 5 a.m.!). The puppy will indicate that he's ready "to go" by circling or sniffing busily—do not misinterpret these signs. For a puppy less than ten weeks of age, a routine of taking him out every hour is necessary. As the puppy grows, he will be able to wait for longer periods of time.

Keep trips to his relief area short. Stay no more than five or six minutes and then return to the house. If he goes during that time, praise him lavishly and take him indoors immediately. If he does not, but he has an accident when you go back indoors, pick him up immediately, say "No! No!" and return to his relief area. Wait a few minutes, then return to the house again. *Never* hit a puppy or put his face in urine or excrement when he has had an accident!

Once indoors, put the puppy in his crate until you have had time to clean up his accident. Then release him to the family area and watch him more closely than before. Chances are, his accident was a result of your not

picking up his signal or waiting too long before offering him the opportunity to relieve himself. Never hold a grudge against the puppy for accidents.

Let the puppy learn that going outdoors means it is time to relieve himself, not to play. Once trained, he will be able to play indoors and out and still differentiate between the times for play versus the times for relief.

Help him develop regular hours for naps, being alone, playing by himself and just resting, all in his crate. Encourage him to entertain himself while you are busy with your activities. Let him learn that having you near is comforting, but it is not your main purpose in life to provide him with undivided attention.

Each time you put your puppy in his own area, use the same command, whatever suits best. Soon he will run to his crate or special area when he

Baby gates, used in the home for a toddler's safety, are equally effective in confining your Newf(s) to a particular room.

THE CLEAN LIFE

By providing sleeping and resting quarters that fit the dog, and offering frequent opportunities to relieve himself outside his quarters, the puppy quickly learns that the outdoors is the place to go when he needs to urinate or defecate. It also reinforces his innate desire to keep his sleeping quarters clean. This, in turn, helps develop the muscle control that will eventually produce a dog with clean living habits.

hears you say those words. Crate training provides safety for you, the puppy and the home. It also provides the puppy with a feeling of security, and that helps the puppy achieve self-confidence and clean habits.

Remember that one of the primary ingredients in house-training your puppy is control. Regardless of your lifestyle, there will always be occasions when you will need to have a place where your dog can stay and be

THE SUCCESS METHOD

Success that comes by luck is usually short-lived. Success that comes by well-thought-out proven methods is often more easily achieved and permanent. This is the Success Method. It is designed to give you, the puppy owner, a simple yet proven way to help your puppy develop clean living habits and a feeling of security in his new environment.

6 Steps to Successful Crate Training

1 Tell the puppy "Crate time!" and place him in the crate with a small treat (a piece of cheese or half of a biscuit). Let him stay in the crate for five minutes while you are in the same room. Then release him and praise lavishly. Never release him when he is fussing. Wait until he is quiet before you let him out.

2 Repeat Step 1 several times a day.

3 The next day, place the puppy in the crate as before. Let him stay there for ten minutes. Do this several times.

4 Continue building time in five-minute increments until the puppy stays in his crate for 30 minutes with you in the room. Always take him to his relief area after prolonged periods in his crate.

5 Now go back to Step 1 and let the puppy stay in his crate for five minutes, this time while you are out of the room.

6 Once again, build crate time in five-minute increments with you out of the room. When the puppy will stay willingly in his crate (he may even fall asleep!) for 30 minutes with you out of the room, he will be ready to stay in it for several hours at a time.

happy and safe. Crate training is the answer for now and in the future.

In conclusion, a few key elements are really all you need for a successful house-training method—consistency, frequency, praise, control and supervision. By following these procedures with a normal, healthy puppy, you and the puppy will soon be past the stage of "accidents" and ready to move on to a clean and rewarding life together.

ROLES OF DISCIPLINE, REWARD AND PUNISHMENT

Discipline, training one to act in accordance with rules, brings order to life. It is as simple as that. Without discipline, particularly in a group society, chaos reigns supreme and the group will eventually perish. Humans and canines are social animals and need some form of discipline in order to function effec-

Always clean up after your dog, whether you are in a public place or your own yard.

tively. They must procure food, reproduce to keep the species going and protect their home base and their young.

If there were no discipline in the lives of social animals, they would eventually die from starvation and/or predation by other stronger animals. In the case of domestic canines, dogs need discipline in their lives in order to understand how their pack (you and other family members) functions and how they must act in order to survive.

A large humane society in a highly populated area recently surveyed dog owners regarding their satisfaction with their relationships with their dogs. People who had trained their dogs were 75% more satisfied with their pets than those who had never trained their dogs.

Dr. Edward Thorndike, a noted psychologist, established *Thorndike's Theory of Learning*, which states that a behavior that results in a pleasant event tends to be repeated. A behavior that results in an unpleasant event

---

THE GOLDEN RULE

The golden rule of dog training is simple. For each "question" (command), there is only one correct answer (reaction). One command = one reaction. Keep practicing the command until the dog reacts correctly without hesitating. Be repetitive but not monotonous, and keep the lessons to a few minutes at a time, several times a day. Dogs get bored just as people do!

FAMILY TIES

If you have other pets in the home and/or interact often with the pets of friends and other family members, your dog will respond to those pets in much the same manner as you do. It is only when you show fear of or resentment toward another animal that he will act fearful or unfriendly.

punishment often comes from an outside source. For example, a child is told not to touch the stove because he may get burned. He disobeys and touches the stove. In doing so, he receives a burn. From that time on, he respects the heat of the stove and avoids contact with it. Therefore, a behavior that results in an unpleasant event tends not to be repeated.

A good example of a dog's learning the hard way is the dog who chases the house cat. He is told many times to leave the cat alone, yet he persists in teasing the cat. Then, one day he begins chasing the cat but the cat turns and swipes a claw across the dog's face, leaving him with a painful gash on his nose. The final result is that the dog stops chasing the cat.

TRAINING EQUIPMENT

COLLAR AND LEAD

For a Newfoundland, the collar and lead that you use for training must be one with which you are easily able to work, not too heavy for the dog and perfectly safe.

TREATS

Have a bag of treats on hand. Something nutritious and easy to swallow works best. Use a soft treat, a chunk of cheese or a piece of cooked chicken rather

tends not to be repeated. It is this theory on which training methods are based today. For example, if you manipulate a dog to perform a specific behavior and reward him for doing it, he is likely to do it again because he enjoyed the end result.

Occasionally, punishment, a penalty inflicted for an offense, is necessary. The best type of than a dry biscuit. By the time the dog has finished chewing a dry treat, he will forget why he is being rewarded in the first place! Using food rewards will not teach a dog to beg at the table—the only way to teach a dog to beg at the table is to give him food from the table. In training, rewarding the dog with a food treat will help him associate praise and the treats with learning new behaviors that obviously please his owner.

TRAINING BEGINS: ASK THE DOG A QUESTION

In order to teach your dog anything, you must first get his attention. After all, he cannot learn anything if he is looking away from you with his mind on something else.

To get his attention, ask him "School?" and immediately walk over to him and give him a treat as you tell him "Good dog." Wait a minute or two and repeat the routine, this time with a treat in your hand as you approach within a foot of the dog. Do not go directly to him, but stop about a foot short of him and hold out the treat as you ask "School?" He will see you approaching with a treat in your hand and most likely begin walking toward you. As you meet, give him the treat and praise again.

The third time, ask the question, have a treat in your hand

TRAINING RULES

If you want to be successful in training your dog, you have four rules to obey yourself:

1. Develop an understanding of how a dog thinks.
2. Do not blame the dog for lack of communication.
3. Define your dog's personality and act accordingly.
4. Have patience and be consistent.

READY, SIT, GO!

On your marks, get set: train! Most professional trainers agree that the sit command is the place to start your dog's formal education. Sitting is a natural posture for most dogs and they respond to the sit exercise willingly and readily. For every lesson, begin with the sit command, so that you start out with a successful exercise. Likewise, you should practice the sit command at the end of every lesson as well because you always want to end on a high note.

and walk only a short distance toward the dog so that he must walk almost all the way to you. As he reaches you, give him the treat and praise again.

By this time, the dog will probably be getting the idea that if he pays attention to you, especially when you ask that question, it will pay off in treats and enjoyable activities for him. In other words, he learns that "school" means doing great things with you that are fun and result in positive attention for him.

Remember that the dog does not understand your verbal language; he only recognizes sounds. Your question translates to a series of sounds for him, and those sounds become the signal to go to you and pay attention; if he does, he will get to interact with you plus receive treats and praise.

THE BASIC COMMANDS

TEACHING SIT

Now that you have the dog's attention, attach his lead and hold it in your left hand and a food treat in your right. Place your food hand at the dog's nose and let him lick the treat but not take it from you. Say "Sit" and slowly raise your food hand from in front of the dog's nose up over his head so that he is looking at the ceiling. As he bends his head upward, he will have to bend his knees to maintain his balance. As he bends his knees, he will assume a sit position. At that point, release the food treat and praise lavishly with comments such as "Good dog! Good sit!," etc. Remember to always praise enthusiastically, because dogs relish verbal praise from their owners and feel so proud of themselves whenever they accomplish a behavior.

You will not use food forever in getting the dog to obey your commands. Food is only used to teach new behaviors, and once the dog knows what you want when you give a specific command, you will wean him off the food treats but still maintain the verbal praise. After all, you will always have your voice with you, and there will be many times when you have no food rewards but expect the dog to obey.

TEACHING DOWN

Teaching the down exercise is easy when you understand how the dog perceives the down position, and it is very difficult when you do not. Dogs perceive the down position as a submissive one; therefore, teaching the down exercise using a forceful method can sometimes make the dog develop such a fear of the down that he either runs away when you say "Down" or he attempts to snap at the person who tries to force him down.

Have the dog sit close along-side your left leg, facing in the same direction as you are. Hold the lead in your left hand and a food treat in your right. Now

COMMAND STANCE

Stand up straight and authoritatively when giving your dog commands. Do not issue commands when lying on the floor or lying on your back on the sofa. If you are on your hands and knees when you give a command, your dog will think you are positioning yourself to play.

place your left hand lightly on the top of the dog's shoulders where they meet above the spinal cord. Do not push down on the dog's shoulders; simply rest your left hand there so you can guide the dog to lie down close to your left leg rather than to swing away from your side when he drops.

DOUBLE JEOPARDY

A dog in jeopardy never lies down. He stays alert on his feet because instinct tells him that he may have to run away or fight for his survival. Therefore, if a dog feels threatened or anxious, he will not lie down. Consequently, it is important to keep the dog calm and relaxed as he learns the down exercise.

Now place the food hand at the dog's nose, say "Down" very softly (almost a whisper) and slowly lower the food hand to the dog's front feet. When the food hand reaches the floor, begin moving it forward along the floor in front of the dog. Keep talking softly to the dog, saying things like, "Do you want this treat? You can do this, good dog." Your reassuring tone of voice will help calm the dog as he tries to follow the food hand in order to get the treat.

When the dog's elbows touch the floor, release the food and praise softly. Try to get the dog to maintain that down position for several seconds before you let him sit up again. The goal here is to get the dog to settle down and not feel threatened in the down position.

TEACHING STAY

It is easy to teach the dog to stay in either a sit or a down position. Again, we use food and praise during the teaching process as we help the dog to understand exactly what it is that we are expecting him to do.

To teach the sit/stay, start with the dog sitting on your left side as before and hold the lead in your left hand. Have a food treat in your right hand and place your food hand at the dog's nose. Say "Stay" and step out on your right foot to stand directly in front of the dog, toe to toe, as he licks and nibbles the treat. Be sure to keep his head facing upward to maintain the sit position. Count to five and then swing around to stand next to the dog again with him on your left. As soon as you get back to the original position, release the food and praise lavishly.

To teach the down/stay, do the down as previously described. As soon as the dog lies down, say "Stay" and step out on your right foot just as you did in the sit/stay. Count to five and then return to stand beside the dog with him on your left side. Release the treat and praise as always.

Within a week or ten days, you can begin to add a bit of distance between you and your dog when you leave him. When

A hug for a job well done is as rewarding and satisfying as any treat.

you do, use your left hand open with the palm facing the dog as a stay signal, much the same as the hand signal a police officer uses to stop traffic at an intersection. Hold the food treat in your right hand as before, but this time the food is not touching the dog's nose. He will watch the food hand and quickly learn that he is going to get that treat as soon as you return to his side.

When you can stand 3 feet away from your dog for 30 seconds, you can then begin building time and distance in both stays. Eventually, the dog can be expected to remain in the stay position for prolonged periods of time until you return to him or call him to you. Always praise lavishly when he stays.

LANGUAGE BARRIER

Dogs do not understand our language and have to rely on tone of voice more than just words or sound. They can be trained to react to a certain sound, at a certain volume. If you say "No, Oliver" in a very soft, pleasant voice, it will not have the same meaning as "No, Oliver!!" when you raise your voice.

You should never use the dog's name during a reprimand, just the command "No! " You never want the dog to associate his name with a negative experience or reprimand.

The rewards of training your Newfoundland are long-lasting. An obedient Newf makes for a happy and fulfilling dog/owner relationship.

TEACHING COME

If you make teaching "come" an exciting experience, you should never have a student that does not love the game or that fails to come when called. The secret, it seems, is never to teach the word "come."

At times when an owner most wants his dog to come when called, the owner is likely to be upset or anxious and he allows these feelings to come through in the tone of his voice when he calls his dog. Hearing that desperation in his owner's voice, the dog fears the results of going to him and therefore either disobeys outright or runs in the opposite direction. The secret, therefore, is to teach the dog a game and, when you want him to come to you, simply play the game. It is practically a no-fail solution!

To begin, have several members of your family take a few food treats and each go into a different room in the house. Take turns calling the dog, and each person should celebrate the dog's finding him with a treat and lots of happy praise. When a person calls the dog, he is actually inviting the dog to find him and get a treat as a reward for "winning."

A few turns of the "Where are you?" game and the dog will understand that everyone is playing the game and that each person has a big celebration awaiting his success at locating them. Once the dog learns to love the game, simply calling out "Where are you?" will bring him running from wherever he is when he hears that all-important question.

FEAR AGGRESSION

Pups who are subjected to physical abuse during training commonly end up with behavioral problems as adults. One common result of abuse is fear aggression, in which a dog will lash out, bare his teeth, snarl and finally bite someone by whom he feels threatened. For example, your daughter may be playing with the dog one afternoon. As they play hide-and-seek, she backs the dog into a corner and, as she attempts to tease him playfully, he bites her hand. Examine the cause of this behavior. Did your daughter ever hit the dog? Did someone who resembles your daughter hit or scream at the dog?

Fortunately, fear aggression is relatively easy to correct. Have your daughter engage in only positive activities with the dog, such as feeding, petting and walking. She should not give any corrections or negative feedback. If the dog still growls or cowers away from her, allow someone else to accompany them. After approximately one week, the dog should feel that he can rely on her for many positive things, and he will also be prevented from reacting fearfully towards anyone who might resemble her.

The down-stay command can be accomplished by using a combination of a hand signal and a voice command.

The come command is recognized as one of the most important things to teach a dog, but

CONSISTENCY PAYS OFF
Dogs need consistency in their feeding schedule, exercise and relief visits, and in the verbal commands you use. If you use "Stay" on Monday and "Stay here, please" on Tuesday, you will confuse your dog. Don't demand perfect behavior during training sessions and then let him have the run of the house the rest of the day. Above all, lavish praise on your pet consistently every time he does something right. The more he feels he is pleasing you, the more willing he will be to learn.

there are trainers who work with thousands of dogs and never teach the actual word "come." Yet these dogs will race to respond to a person who uses the dog's name followed by "Where are you?" For example, a woman has a 10-year-old companion dog who went blind, but who never fails to locate her owner when asked, "Where are you?"

Children, in particular, love to play this game with their dogs. Children can hide in smaller places like a shower stall or a bath-tub, behind a bed or under a table. The dog needs to work a little bit harder to find these hiding places, but, when he does, he loves to celebrate with a treat and a tussle with a favorite youngster.

TEACHING HEEL

Heeling means that the dog walks beside the owner without pulling. It takes time and patience on the owner's part to succeed at teaching the dog that he (the owner) will not proceed unless the dog is walking calmly beside him. Pulling out ahead on the lead or lagging behind is definitely not acceptable.

Begin by holding the lead in your left hand as the dog sits beside your left leg. Move the loop end of the lead to your right hand but keep your left hand short on the lead so it keeps the dog in close next to you.

Say "Heel" and step forward on your left foot. Keep the dog close to you and take three steps. Stop and have the dog sit next to you in what we now call the heel position. Praise verbally, but do not touch the dog. Hesitate a moment and begin again with "Heel," taking three steps and stopping, at which point the dog is told to sit again.

Your goal here is to have the dog walk those three steps with-

Once the Newf accepts the idea of finding his owner when asked "Where are you?", he usually will come consistently when called.

out pulling on the lead. Once he will walk calmly beside you for three steps without pulling, increase the number of steps you take to five. When he will walk politely beside you while you take five steps, you can increase the length of your walk to ten steps. Keep increasing the length of your stroll until the dog will walk quietly beside you without pulling as long as you want him to heel. When you stop heeling, indicate to the dog that the exercise is over by verbally praising as you pet him and say "OK, good dog." The "OK" is used as a release word, meaning that the exercise is finished and the dog is free to relax.

When walking a dog the size of the Newfoundland, it is more than sensible to invest the time in training him to heel. A Newf that heels on lead can be walked daily with no problem. An untrained Newf, however, will likely take you for a walk!

If you are dealing with a dog who insists on pulling you around, simply "put on your brakes" and stand your ground

> **"COME" . . . BACK**
> Never call your dog to come to you for a correction or scold him when he reaches you. That is the quickest way to turn a come command into "Go away fast!" Dogs think only in the present tense, and your dog will connect the scolding with coming to you, not with the misbehavior of a few moments earlier.

until the dog realizes that the two of you are not going anywhere until he is beside you and moving at your pace, not his. It may take some time just standing there to convince the dog that you are the leader and you will be the one to decide on the direction and speed of your travel.

Each time the dog looks up at you or slows down to give a slack lead between the two of you, quietly praise him and say, "Good heel. Good dog." Eventually, the dog will begin to respond and within a few days he will be walking politely beside you without pulling on the lead. At first, the training sessions should be kept short and very positive; soon the dog will be able to walk nicely with you for increasingly longer distances. Remember also to give the dog free time and the opportunity to run and play when you have finished heel practice.

WEANING OFF FOOD IN TRAINING

Food is used in training new behaviors. Once the dog understands what behavior goes with a specific command, it is time to start weaning him off the food treats. At first, give a treat after each exercise. Then, start to give a treat only after every other exercise. Mix up the times when you offer a food reward and the times when you offer only praise so that the dog will never know when he is going to receive both food and praise and when he is going to receive only praise. This is called a variable-ratio reward system and it proves successful because there is always the chance that the owner will produce a treat, so the dog never stops trying for that reward. No matter what, *always* give verbal praise.

OBEDIENCE CLASSES

It is a good idea to enroll in an obedience class if one is available in your area. If yours is a show dog, handling classes would be more appropriate. Many areas have dog clubs that offer basic obedience training as well as preparatory classes for obedience competition. There are also local dog trainers who offer similar classes.

At dog shows, dogs can earn titles at various levels of competition. The beginning levels of

> **TUG OF WALK?**
> If you begin teaching the heel by taking long walks and letting the dog pull you along, he misinterprets this action as an acceptable form of taking a walk. When you pull back on the leash to counteract his pulling, he reads that tug as a signal to pull even harder!

competition include basic behaviors such as sit, down, heel, etc. The more advanced levels of competition include jumping, retrieving, scent discrimination and signal work. The advanced levels require a dog and owner to put a lot of time and effort into their training, and the titles that can be earned at these levels of competition are very prestigious.

OTHER ACTIVITIES FOR LIFE

Whether a dog is trained in the structured environment of a class or alone with his owner at home, there are many activities that can bring fun and rewards to both owner and dog once they have mastered basic control.

CONFORMATION SHOWING

If you are interested in exploring the world of dog showing, your best bet is to join your local breed club or the national parent club, which is the Newfoundland Club of America. To locate the breed club closest to you, contact the American Kennel Club (AKC), which furnishes the rules and regulations for all of these events plus general dog registration and other basic requirements of dog ownership.

In the US, the AKC offers three kinds of conformation shows: an all-breed show (for all AKC-recognized breeds), a specialty show (for one breed only, usually sponsored by the parent club) and a Group show (for all breeds in the group). At any dog show, only one dog and one bitch of each breed can win points. Dog showing does not offer "co-ed" classes. Dogs and bitches never compete against each other in the classes. Non-champion dogs are called "class dogs" because they compete in one of five classes. Dogs are entered in a particular class depending on age and previous show wins.

The judge at the show begins judging the Puppy Class, first dogs and then bitches, and proceeds through the classes. The judge places his winners first through fourth in each class. In the Winners Class, the first-place winners of each class compete with one another to determine Winners Dog and

> ### HEELING WELL
> Teach your dog to heel in an enclosed area. Once you think the dog will obey reliably and you want to attempt advanced obedience exercises such as off-lead heeling, test him in a fenced-in area so he cannot run away.

Winners Bitch. The judge also places a Reserve Winners Dog and Reserve Winners Bitch, which could be awarded the points in the case of a disqualification. The Winners Dog and Winners Bitch are the two that are awarded the points for the breed, then compete with any champions of record (often called "specials") entered in the show. The judge reviews the Winners Dog, Winners Bitch and all of the champions to select his Best of Breed. The Best of Winners is selected between the Winners Dog and Winners Bitch. Were one of these two to be selected Best of Breed, he or she would automatically be named Best of Winners as well. Finally the judge selects his Best of Opposite Sex to the Best of Breed winner.

At a Group show or all-breed show, the Best of Breed winners from each breed then compete against one another for Group One through Group Four. The judge compares each Best of Breed to his breed standard, and the dog that most closely lives up to the ideal for his breed is selected as Group One. Finally, all seven group winners (from the Working Group, Toy Group, Hound Group, etc.) compete for Best in Show.

Only unaltered dogs can be entered in a dog show, so if you have spayed or neutered your

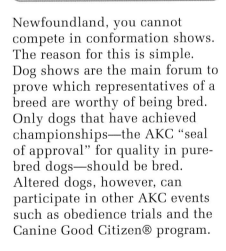

BECOMING A CHAMPION
An official AKC champion of record requires that a dog accumulate 15 points under three different judges, including two "majors" under different judges. Points are awarded based on the number of dogs entered into competition, varying from breed to breed and place to place. A win of three, four or five points is considered a "major." The AKC annually assigns a schedule of points to adjust to the variations that accompany a breed's popularity and the population of a given area.

Newfoundland, you cannot compete in conformation shows. The reason for this is simple. Dog shows are the main forum to prove which representatives of a breed are worthy of being bred. Only dogs that have achieved championships—the AKC "seal of approval" for quality in pure-bred dogs—should be bred. Altered dogs, however, can participate in other AKC events such as obedience trials and the Canine Good Citizen® program.

WATER WORK
The Newfoundland's physical structure, love of water and great affinity for work make him a natural candidate for water activities that are fun for both the dog and his human family. Whether he is working in a water trial or

training for water rescue work, towing a small boat or retrieving objects from the water, the Newf will thrill his human with his enthusiasm for the job at hand.

Training a Newf for water activities is best started at an early age. A proper introduction to water is the best insurance that the dog will develop a happy and confident attitude toward water work. There are many different philosophies on how to ensure that the Newf adapts readily to water and develops a correct swimming

AKC GROUPS
For showing purposes, the American Kennel Club divides its recognized breeds into seven groups: Working Dogs, Sporting Dogs, Hounds, Terriers, Toys, Non-Sporting Dogs and Herding Dogs.

stroke. The handler must be gentle, encouraging and supportive to make sure that the dog is comfortable and unafraid. Keep the lessons fun and simple, building on the dog's skills as he

Dog shows are a popular venue for the Newfoundland, who is a natural beauty and showman. These Newfs and their owners are participating in a specialty show, a contest for only their breed.

This handsome Newfoundland is prepping for his victory photo after an impressive win at a large show.

masters them. Make sure that the dog is rewarded for his progress and try to end each lesson with success. Never train so long that the dog becomes bored and tires of the exercises. Stop training while the dog is still enthusiastic so that he will look forward eagerly to his next training session.

Conduct your training sessions in as many varied water settings as possible. Even if you must travel to find new water, the dog will benefit from the experience of different sites and conditions. Lakes, rivers and, of course, the sea are excellent training locations. Always check with local authorities about natural hazards, tides and currents, and other possible dangers. Be especially conscious of foul weather. If at all possible, join a training group. Not only is it safer and more fun to work your dog with others who are aficionados of the breed but you also gain the benefit of their knowledge and expertise.

For those who would like to pursue organized or formal water competition with their dogs, Newfoundland water tests are offered in many countries. For example, water trials on several levels of difficulty have been offered in Britain since 1964. England's Northern Newfoundland Club was the first organization to form a committee to support a working group. Formal test rules were established on five levels by Paul and Christine Tedder, together with Elaine and Philip Messer, and the Northern Newfoundland Club held the first tests under those rules in 1990. That year, the Newfoundland Club also set up a working committee and, since that time, both clubs have held at least three water tests each year. In 1994, revised water test regulations were agreed upon by both clubs, and current tests now follow the revised rules.

In the United States, the Newfoundland Club of America

FIVE CLASSES AT SHOWS

At most AKC all-breed shows, there are five regular classes offered: Puppy, Novice, Bred-by-Exhibitor, American-bred and Open. The Puppy Class is usually divided as 6 to 9 months of age and 9 to 12 months of age. When deciding in which class to enter your dog, male or female, you must carefully check the show schedule to make sure that you have selected the right class. Depending on the age of the dog, previous first-place wins and the sex of the dog, you must make the best choice. It is possible to enter a one-year-old dog who has not won sufficient first places in any of the non-Puppy Classes, though the competition is more intense the further you progress from the Puppy Class.

offers the working title of WRD-NCA (Working Rescue Dog-Newfoundland Club of America) that appears after the dog's name. NCA water tests are divided into Junior and Senior levels and have become so popular that the Newfoundland Club of Denmark has adopted a water training program based on NCA exercises.

Canada also offers the water-work titles of WRD and WRDX to dogs who win the Junior and Senior exercises held in that country. Internationally, water trials are held in countries where breed popularity is strong enough to support a working breed club.

AGILITY TRIALS

If you are interested in participating in organized competition with your Newfoundland, there are activities other than obedience and water trials in which you and your dog can become involved. Agility is a popular sport where dogs run through an obstacle course that includes various jumps, tunnels and other exercises to test the dogs' speed and coordination. The owners run beside their dogs to give commands and to guide them through the course. Although competitive, the focus is on fun—it's fun to do, fun to watch and great exercise.

Whether you are working your Newfoundland in water tests or simply exercising him in the surf, your loving Newf will be happy to participate.

Although the Newf is a natural swimmer, training the dog for water rescue requires specialized handling.

When a year old, the Newf is outfitted with life-saving gear to which he must become acclimated.

Once acclimated, the Newf is able to swim uninhibitedly with his gear in place.

An inspiring moment in water training is seeing the dog respond to a "person in distress." This Newf is practicing a save on a stuffed rubber suit.

Towing a life raft by grasping a handle and swimming toward shore, this Newf is proving a true lifesaver.

Newfs were bred for generations for water rescue, and a properly trained Newf will revel in the opportunity to respond to a call for help.

Agility trials have become popular around the world. At an agility trial, this Newf is maneuvering over the see-saw obstacle with guidance from his handler.

TRACKING

Any dog is capable of tracking, using his nose to follow a trail. Tracking tests are exciting and competitive ways to test your Newfoundland's instinctive scenting ability and his ability to search and rescue. The AKC started tracking tests in 1937, when the first AKC-licensed test took place as part of the Utility level at an obedience trial. Ten years later in 1947, the AKC offered the first title, Tracking Dog (TD). It was not until 1980 that the AKC added the title Tracking Dog Excellent (TDX), which was followed by the title Versatile Surface Tracking (VST) in 1995. The title Champion Tracker (CT) is awarded to a dog who has earned all three titles.

CARTING, BACKPACKING AND BEYOND

Teaching the dog to help out around the home, in the yard or on the farm provides great satisfaction to both dog and owner. In addition, the dog's help makes life

DRAFT TESTS

Another original purpose of the breed was as a draft dog, and the NCA's draft tests judge the dog's ability to work with his handler and complete tasks, thus demonstrating that he would be able to perform well in actual work situations. Since draft work is a team effort between dog and handler, the handler must also have a grasp on the work involved as well as be able to control the dog and work with the necessary equipment.

Newfoundlands have been successfully trained as carting dogs. This Newf is in training with an empty cart. To prevent strain and injury, it is important not to overload a cart beyond the dog's ability.

a little easier for his owner and raises his stature as a valued companion to his family. It helps give the dog a purpose by occupying his mind and providing an outlet for his energy.

Backpacking is an exciting and healthy activity that the dog can be taught without assistance from more than his owner. The exercise of walking and climbing is good for man and dog alike, and the bond that they develop together is priceless. The rule for backpacking with any dog is never to expect the dog to carry more than one-sixth of his body weight.

Carting is another activity at which the Newf excels, as do many other large-breed dogs. Training for cart-pulling is also ideal for the Newf whose owner needs a helper around the yard.

There are clubs associated with the kennel clubs that are dedicated to carting. An experienced carting person should be contacted to be sure that you purchase the right cart for your Newf. Additionally, the distribution of weight on the cart is a critical consideration. Beyond being a great help in your gardening and outdoor chores, carting can be great fun for Newf and owner as well.

Another positive advantage to the Newfoundland: he can provide lots of fun for the children, a chore the Newf welcomes with enthusiasm. Be sure to monitor your dog whenever he is with children.

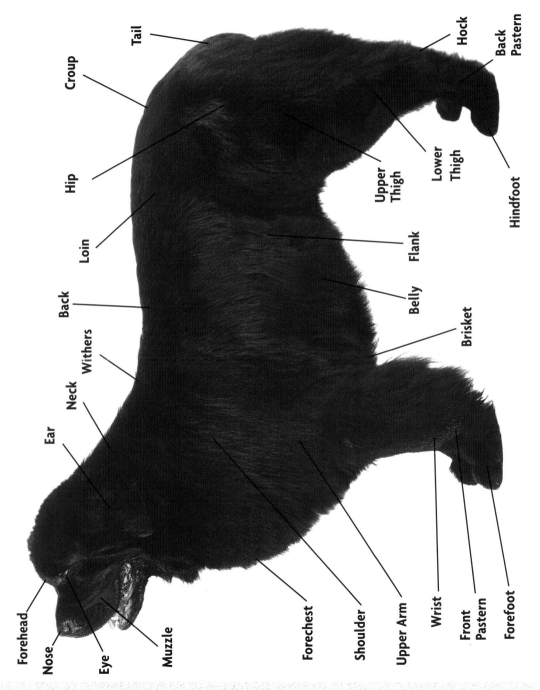

PHYSICAL STRUCTURE OF THE NEWFOUNDLAND

HEALTH CARE OF YOUR

NEWFOUNDLAND

Dogs suffer many of the same physical illnesses as people. They might even share many of the same psychological problems. Since people usually know more about human diseases than canine maladies, many of the terms used in this chapter will be familiar but not necessarily those used by veterinarians. We will use the term *x-ray*, instead of the more acceptable term *radiograph*. We will also use the familiar term *symptoms* even though dogs don't have symptoms, which are verbal descriptions of the patient's feelings; dogs have *clinical signs*. Since dogs can't speak, we have to look for clinical signs...but we still use the term *symptoms* here.

As a general rule, medicine is *practiced*. That term is not arbitrary. Medicine is a constantly changing art as we learn more and more about genetics, electronic aids (like CAT scans and MRIs) and daily laboratory advances. There are many dog maladies, like canine hip dysplasia, which are not universally treated in the same manner. For example, some veterinarians opt for surgical treatments more often than others.

SELECTING A VETERINARIAN

Your selection of a veterinarian should be based upon his personality and skills with large-breed dogs, as well as upon his convenience to your home. You want a vet who is close because you might have emergencies or need to make multiple visits for treatments. You want a vet who has services that you might require such as tattooing and boarding facilities, and of course a good reputation for ability and responsiveness. There is nothing more frustrating than having to wait a day or more to get a response from your veterinarian.

All veterinarians are licensed and should be capable of dealing with your dog's health maintenance, routine care, illnesses, injuries and the like. Most vets do routine surgery such as neutering, stitching up wounds and docking tails for those breeds in which such is required for show purposes. There are, however, many veterinary specialties that require further studies and internships. These include specialists in heart prob-

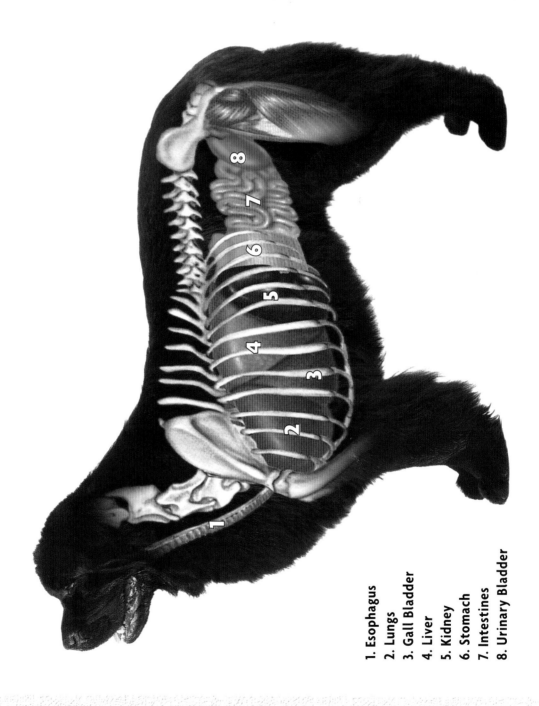

1. Esophagus
2. Lungs
3. Gall Bladder
4. Liver
5. Kidney
6. Stomach
7. Intestines
8. Urinary Bladder

INTERNAL ORGANS OF THE NEWFOUNDLAND

lems (veterinary cardiologists), skin problems (veterinary dermatologists), tooth and gum problems (veterinary dentists), eye problems (veterinary ophthalmologists) and x-rays (veterinary radiologists), as well as vets who have specialties in bones, muscles or certain organs.

When the problem affecting your dog is serious, it is not unusual or impudent to get another medical opinion, although it is wise and courteous to advise the vets concerned about this. You might also want to compare costs among several veterinarians. Sophisticated health care and veterinary

Breakdown of Veterinary Income by Category

%	Category
2%	Dentistry
4%	Radiology
12%	Surgery
15%	Vaccinations
19%	Laboratory
23%	Examinations
25%	Medicines

A typical vet's income, categorized according to services performed. This survey dealt with small-animal (pets) practices.

services can be very costly. It is not infrequent that important decisions about which treatment route to take are based upon financial considerations.

PREVENTATIVE MEDICINE

It is much easier, less costly and more effective to practice preventative medicine than to fight bouts of illness and disease. Properly bred puppies come from parents who were selected based upon their genetic-disease profiles. Their mothers should have been vaccinated, free of all internal and external parasites and properly nourished. For these reasons, a visit to the veterinarian who cared for the dam is recommended. The dam can pass on disease resistance to her puppies, which can last for eight to ten weeks. She can also pass on parasites and many

DENTAL HEALTH

A dental examination is in order when the dog is between six months and one year of age so that any permanent teeth that have erupted incorrectly can be corrected. It is important to begin a brushing routine at home, using dental-care products made for dogs, such as special toothbrushes and canine toothpaste. Durable nylon and safe edible chews should be a part of your Newf's arsenal for good health, good teeth and pleasant breath. The vast majority of dogs three to four years old and older has diseases of the gums from lack of dental attention. Using the various types of dental chews can be very effective in controlling dental plaque.

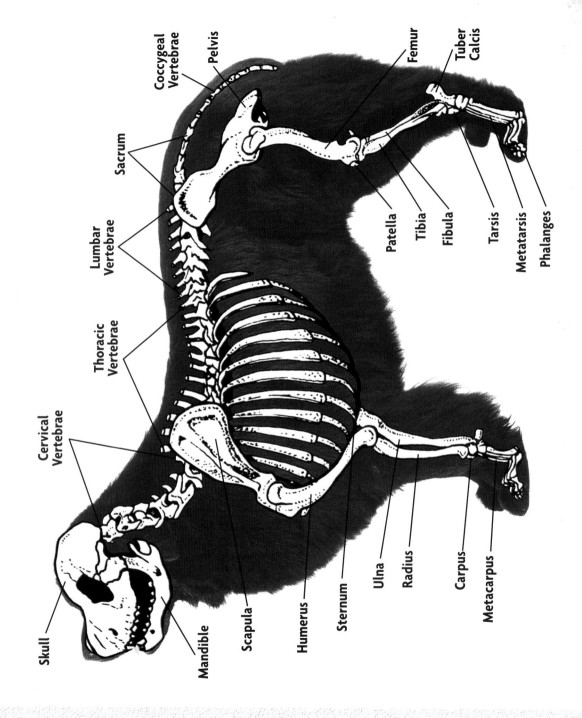

SKELETAL STRUCTURE OF THE NEWFOUNDLAND

"P" STANDS FOR PROBLEM
Urinary-tract disease is a serious condition that requires immediate medical attention. Symptoms include urinating in inappropriate places or the need to urinate frequently in small amounts. Urinary-tract disease is most effectively treated with antibiotics. To help promote good urinary-tract health, owners must always be sure that a constant supply of fresh water is available to their pets.

infections. That's why it's helpful to know as much about the dam's health as possible.

VACCINATION SCHEDULING
Most vaccinations are given by injection and should only be done by a veterinarian. Both he and you should keep a record of the date of the injection, the identification of the vaccine and the amount given. Some vets give a first vaccination at six weeks, but most dog breeders prefer the course not to commence until about eight weeks because of a risk of negating any antibodies passed on by the dam. The vaccination scheduling is usually based on a two- to four-week cycle. You must take your vet's advice regarding when to vaccinate as this may differ according to the vaccine used.

Most vaccinations immunize your puppy against viruses. The usual vaccines contain immunizing doses of several different viruses such as distemper, parvovirus, parainfluenza and hepatitis, although some veterinarians recommend separate vaccines for each disease. There are other vaccines available when the puppy is at risk. You should rely upon professional advice. This is especially true for the booster-shot program. Most vaccination programs require a booster when the puppy is a year old and once a year thereafter. In some cases, circumstances may require more or less frequent immunizations.

Canine cough, more formally known as tracheobronchitis, is treated with a vaccine that is sprayed into the dog's nostrils. Canine cough is usually included in routine vaccination, but this is often not as effective as the vaccines for other major diseases.

WEANING TO BRINGING PUPPY HOME
Puppies should be weaned by the time they are about two months old. A puppy that remains for at least eight weeks with his mother and littermates usually adapts better to other dogs and people later in his life.

Sometimes new owners have their puppy examined by a veterinarian immediately, which is a good idea, unless the pup is overtired by the journey home from the breeder. In that case, an

HEALTH AND VACCINATION SCHEDULE

AGE IN WEEKS:	6TH	8TH	10TH	12TH	14TH	16TH	20-24TH	52ND
Worm Control	✔	✔	✔	✔	✔	✔	✔	
Neutering							✔	
Heartworm		✔		✔		✔	✔	
Parvovirus	✔		✔		✔		✔	✔
Distemper		✔		✔		✔		✔
Hepatitis		✔		✔		✔		✔
Leptospirosis								✔
Parainfluenza	✔		✔		✔			✔
Dental Examination		✔					✔	✔
Complete Physical		✔					✔	✔
Coronavirus				✔			✔	✔
Canine Cough	✔							
Hip Dysplasia							✔	
Rabies							✔	

Vaccinations are not instantly effective. It takes about two weeks for the dog's immune system to develop antibodies. Most vaccinations require annual booster shots. Your vet should guide you in this regard.

appointment should be made for the next day.

The puppy will have his teeth examined and have his skeletal conformation and general health checked prior to certification by the veterinarian. Puppies in certain breeds have problems with their kneecaps, cataracts and other eye problems, heart murmurs and undescended testicles. Your veterinarian might also have training in temperament evaluation. At the first visit, the vet will set up a schedule for the pup's vaccinations.

FIVE TO TWELVE MONTHS OF AGE

Unless you intend to breed or show your dog, neutering the puppy around six months of age is recommended. Discuss this with your veterinarian. Neutering/spaying has proven to be extremely beneficial to both male and female dogs. Besides eliminating the possibility of pregnancy and pyometra in bitches and testicular cancer in males, it greatly reduces the risk of (but does not prevent) breast cancer in bitches and prostate cancer in male dogs.

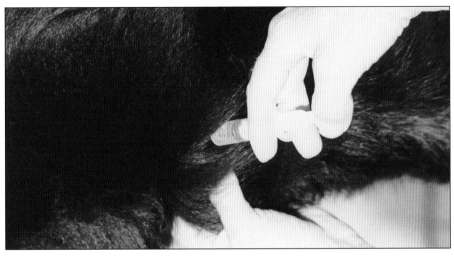

Discuss a vaccination program with your veterinarian. Vaccines should be administered by a qualified vet.

DISEASE REFERENCE CHART

	What is it?	What causes it?	Symptoms
Leptospirosis	Severe disease that affects the internal organs; can be spread to people.	A bacterium, which is often carried by rodents, that enters through mucous membranes and spreads quickly throughout the body.	Range from fever, vomiting and loss of appetite in less severe cases to shock, irreversible kidney damage and possibly death in most severe cases.
Rabies	Potentially deadly virus that infects warm-blooded mammals.	Bite from a carrier of the virus, mainly wild animals.	1st stage: dog exhibits change in behavior, fear. 2nd stage: dog's behavior becomes more aggressive. 3rd stage: loss of coordination, trouble with bodily functions.
Parvovirus	Highly contagious virus, potentially deadly.	Ingestion of the virus, which is usually spread through the feces of infected dogs.	Most common: severe diarrhea. Also vomiting, fatigue, lack of appetite.
Canine cough	Contagious respiratory infection.	Combination of types of bacteria and virus. Most common: *Bordetella bronchiseptica* bacteria and parainfluenza virus.	Chronic cough.
Distemper	Disease primarily affecting respiratory and nervous system.	Virus that is related to the human measles virus.	Mild symptoms such as fever, lack of appetite and mucus secretion progress to evidence of brain damage, "hard pad."
Hepatitis	Virus primarily affecting the liver.	Canine adenovirus type I (CAV-1). Enters system when dog breathes in particles.	Lesser symptoms include listlessness, diarrhea, vomiting. More severe symptoms include "blue-eye" (clumps of virus in eye).
Coronavirus	Virus resulting in digestive problems.	Virus is spread through infected dog's feces.	Stomach upset evidenced by lack of appetite, vomiting, diarrhea.

VACCINE ALLERGIES

Vaccines do not work all the time. Sometimes dogs are allergic to them and many times the antibodies, which are supposed to be stimulated by the vaccine, just are not produced. You should keep your dog in the veterinary clinic for an hour after he is vaccinated to be sure there are no allergic reactions.

Your veterinarian should provide your puppy with a thorough dental evaluation at six months of age, ascertaining whether all of the permanent teeth have erupted properly. A home dental-care regimen should be initiated at six months, including brushing weekly and providing good dental devices (such as nylon bones). Regular dental care promotes healthy teeth, fresh breath and a longer life.

OLDER THAN ONE YEAR
Once a year, your grown dog should visit the vet for an examination and vaccination boosters, if needed. Some vets recommend blood tests, thyroid level check and dental evaluation to accompany these annual visits. A thorough clinical evaluation by the vet can provide critical background information for your dog. Blood tests are often performed starting at one year of age, as well as full dental examinations and possibly tooth scaling. In the long run, quality preventative care for your pet can save money, teeth and lives.

SKIN PROBLEMS IN NEWFOUNDLANDS
Veterinarians are consulted by dog owners for skin problems more than any for other group of diseases or maladies. Dogs' skin is almost as sensitive as human skin and both can suffer from almost the same ailments (though the occurrence of acne in most breeds is rare). For this reason, veterinary dermatology has developed into a specialty practiced by many veterinarians.

Since many skin problems have visual symptoms that are almost identical, it requires the skill of an experienced veterinary dermatologist to identify and cure many of the more severe skin disorders. Pet shops sell many treatments for skin problems, but most of the treatments are directed at symptoms and not the underlying problem(s). If your dog is suffering from a skin disorder, you should seek professional assistance as quickly as possible. As with all diseases, the earlier a problem is identified and treated, the more likely it is that the cure will be successful.

KNOW WHEN TO POSTPONE A VACCINATION

While the visit to the vet is costly, it is never advisable to update a vaccination when visiting with a sick or pregnant dog. Vaccinations should be avoided for all elderly dogs. If your dog is showing the signs of any illness or any medical condition, no matter how serious or mild, including skin irritations, do not vaccinate. Likewise, a lame dog should never be vaccinated; any dog undergoing surgery or on any immuno-suppressant drugs should not be vaccinated until fully recovered.

HEREDITARY SKIN DISORDERS

Veterinary dermatologists are currently researching a number of skin disorders that are believed to have hereditary bases. These inherited diseases are transmitted by both parents, who appear (phenotypically) normal but have a recessive gene for the disease, meaning that they carry, but are not affected by, the disease. These diseases pose serious problems to breeders because in some instances there is no method of identifying carriers. Often the secondary diseases associated with these skin conditions are even more debilitating than the disorder itself, including cancers and respiratory problems.

Among the hereditary skin disorders, for which the mode of

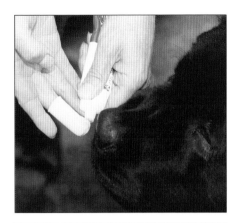

Brushing your Newfoundland's teeth can prevent decay and bad breath. Purchase a doggy toothpaste and applicator or brush at the pet shop. Accustom the pup to tooth cleaning from an early age.

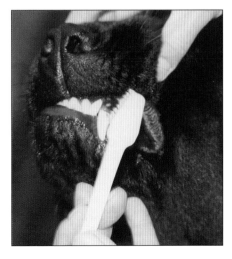

Much can hide in your Newfie's coat, including insects, grasses and other allergens and irritants. Pay close attention to his skin and coat with regular check-overs.

may even become infected. Dogs have the same reaction to fleas, ticks and/or mites. When an insect lands on you, you have the chance to whisk it away with your hand. Unfortunately, when your dog is bitten by a flea, tick or mite, he can only scratch it away or bite it. By the time the dog has been bitten, the parasite has done some of its damage. It may also have laid eggs to cause further problems in the near future. The itching from parasite bites is probably due to the saliva injected into the site when the parasite sucks the dog's blood.

inheritance is known, are acro-dermatitis, cutaneous asthenia (Ehlers-Danlos syndrome), seba-ceous adenitis, cyclic hemato-poiesis, dermatomyositis, IgA deficiency, color dilution alope-cia and nodular dermatofibrosis. Some of these disorders are limited to one or two breeds and others affect a large number of breeds. All inherited diseases must be diagnosed and treated by a veterinary specialist.

PARASITE BITES
Many of us are allergic to insect bites. The bites itch, erupt and

A SKUNKY PROBLEM
Have you noticed your dog dragging his rump along the floor? If so, it is likely that his anal sacs are impacted or possibly infected. The anal sacs are small pouches located on both sides of the anus under the skin and muscles. They are about the size and shape of a grape and contain a foul-smelling liquid. Their contents are usually emptied when the dog has a bowel movement but, if not emptied completely, they will impact, which will cause your dog much pain. Fortunately, your veteri-narian can tend to this problem easily by draining the sacs for the dog. Be aware that your dog might also empty his anal sacs in cases of extreme fright.

The Eyes Have It!

Eye disease is more prevalent among dogs than most people think, ranging from slight infections that are easily treated to serious complications that can lead to permanent sight loss. Eye diseases need veterinary attention in their early stages to prevent irreparable damage. This list provides descriptions of some common eye diseases:

Cataracts: Symptoms are white or gray discoloration of the eye lens and pupil, which causes fuzzy or completely obscured vision. Surgical treatment is required to remove the damaged lens and replace it with an artificial one.

Conjunctivitis: An inflammation of the mucus membrane that lines the eye socket, leaving the eyes red and puffy with excessive discharge. This condition is easily treated with antibiotics.

Corneal damage: The cornea is the transparent covering of the iris and pupil. Injuries are difficult to detect, but manifest themselves in surface abnormality, redness, pain and discharge. Most infections of the cornea are treated with antibiotics and require immediate medical attention.

Dry eye: This condition is caused by deficient production of tears that lubricate and protect the eye surface. A telltale sign is yellow-green discharge. Left undiagnosed, your dog will experience considerable pain, infections and possibly blindness. Dry eye is commonly treated with antibiotics, although more advanced cases may require surgery.

Glaucoma: This is caused by excessive fluid pressure in the eye. Symptoms are red eyes, gray or blue discoloration, pain, enlarged eyeballs and loss of vision. Antibiotics sometimes help, but surgery may be needed.

AUTO-IMMUNE SKIN CONDITIONS

Auto-immune skin conditions are commonly referred to as being allergic to yourself, while allergies are usually inflammatory reactions to an outside stimulus. Auto-immune diseases cause serious damage to the tissues that are involved.

The best known auto-immune disease is lupus, which affects people as well as dogs. The symptoms are variable and may affect the kidneys, bones, blood chemistry and skin. It can be fatal to both dogs and humans, though it is not thought to be transmissible. It is usually successfully treated with cortisone, prednisone or a similar corticosteroid, but extensive use of these drugs can have harmful side effects.

AIRBORNE ALLERGIES

An interesting allergy is pollen allergy. Humans have hay fever, rose fever and other fevers with which they suffer during the pollinating season. Many dogs suffer from the same allergies. When the pollen count is high, your dog might suffer, but don't expect him to sneeze and have a runny nose like a human would. Dogs react to pollen allergies the same way they react to fleas—they scratch and bite themselves.

Dogs, like humans, can be tested for allergens. Discuss the testing with your veterinary dermatologist.

CUSHING'S DISEASE

Cases of hyperactive adrenal glands (Cushing's disease) have been traced to the drinking of highly chlorinated water. Aerate or age your dog's drinking water before offering it.

FOOD PROBLEMS

FOOD ALLERGIES

Dogs can be allergic to many foods that are best-sellers and highly recommended by breeders and vets. Changing the brand of

A healthy Newf is an active and fit dog. If your Newf is lazy, an exercise program is essential to prevent obesity.

Don't Eat the Daisies!

Many plants and flowers are beautiful to look at, but can be highly toxic if ingested by your dog. Reactions range from abdominal pain and vomiting to convulsions and death. If the following plants are in your home, remove them. If they are outside your house or in your garden, avoid accidents by making sure your dog is never left unsupervised in those locations.

Azalea	Dumb cane	Mescal bean
Belladonna	Dutchman's breeches	Mushrooms
Bird of paradise	Elephant's ear	Nightshade
Bulbs	Hydrangea	Philodendron
Calla lily	Jack-in-the-pulpit	Poinsettia
Cardinal flower	Jasmine	*Prunus* species
Castor bean	Jimsonweed	Tobacco
Chinaberry tree	Larkspur	Yellow jasmine
Daphne	Laurel	Yews, *Taxus* species
	Lily of the valley	

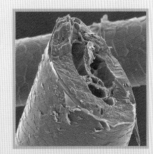
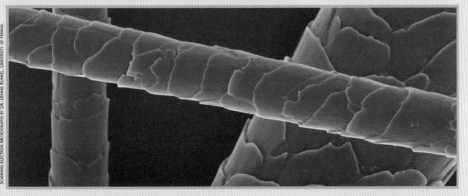

Normal hairs of a dog enlarged 200 times original size. The cuticle (outer covering) is clean and healthy. Unlike human hair that grows from the base, a dog's hair also grows from the end. Damaged hairs and split ends, illustrated above.

SCANNING ELECTRON MICROGRAPHS BY DR. DENNIS KUNKEL, UNIVERSITY OF HAWAII.

HOW TO PREVENT BLOAT

Research has confirmed that the structure of deep-chested breeds contributes to their predisposition to bloat. Nevertheless, there are simple precautions that you can take to reduce the risk of this condition:

- Feed your dog twice daily rather than offer one big meal;
- Do not exercise your dog for at least one hour before and two hours after he has eaten;
- Make certain that your dog is calm and not overly excited while he is eating. It has been proven that nervous or overly excited dogs are more prone to develop bloat;
- Add a small portion of moist meat product to his dry food ration;
- Serve his meals and water in an elevated bowl stand, which avoids the dog's craning his neck to reach his bowls;
- To prevent your dog from gobbling his food too quickly, and thereby swallowing air, put some large (unswallowable) toys into his bowl so that he will have to eat around them to get his food;
- Never allow him to gulp water.

food that you buy may not eliminate the problem if the element to which the dog is allergic is contained in the new brand.

Recognizing a food allergy can be difficult. Humans often have rashes when they eat foods to which they are allergic, or have swelling of the lips or eyes. Dogs do not usually develop rashes, but react in the same way as they to an airborne or bite allergy—they itch, scratch and bite. While pollen allergies and parasite bites are usually seasonal, pollen allergies are year-round problems.

TREATING FOOD ALLERGY

Diagnosis of food allergy is based on a two- to four-week dietary trial with a home-cooked diet fed to the exclusion of all other foods. The diet should consist of boiled rice or potato with a source of protein that the dog has never eaten before, such as fresh or frozen fish, lamb or another quality animal protein source. Water has to be the only drink, and it is really important that no other foods are fed during this trial. If the dog's condition improves, you will need to try the original diet once again to see if the itching resumes. If it does, then this confirms the diagnosis that the dog is allergic to his original diet. The treatment is long-term feeding of something that does not distress the dog's skin, which may

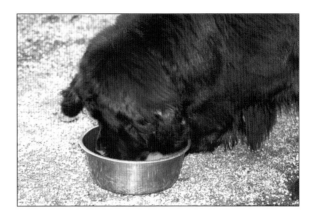

DETECTING BLOAT

As important as it is to take precautions against bloat/gastric torsion, it is of equal importance to recognize the symptoms. It is necessary for your Newfie to get immediate veterinary attention if you notice any of the following signs:

• Your dog's stomach starts to distend, ending up large and as tight as a football;

• Your dog is dribbling, as no saliva can be swallowed;

• Your dog makes frequent attempts to vomit but cannot bring anything up due to the stomach's being closed off;

• Your dog is distressed from pain;

• Your dog starts to suffer from clinical shock, meaning that there is not enough blood in the dog's circulation as the hard, dilated stomach stops the blood from returning to the heart to be pumped around the body. Clinical shock is indicated by pale gums and tongue, as they have been starved of blood. The shocked dog also has glazed, staring eyes.

You have minutes, yes *minutes*, to get your dog into surgery. If you see any of these symptoms at any time of the day or night, get to the vet immediately. Someone will have to phone and warn that you are on your way (which is a justification for the invention of the cellular phone!) so that they can be prepared to get your pet on the operating table right away.

be in the form of one of the commercially available hypoallergenic diets or the home-made diet that you created for the allergy trial.

FOOD INTOLERANCE

Food intolerance is the inability of the dog to completely digest certain foods. This occurs because the dog does not have the chemicals necessary to digest some foodstuffs. These chemicals are called enzymes. All puppies have the enzymes necessary to digest canine milk, but some dogs do not have the enzymes to digest a very different form of milk that is commonly found in human households—milk from cows. In such dogs, drinking cows' milk results in loose bowels, stomach pains and the passage of gas.

Dogs often do not have the enzymes to digest Soy or other beans. The treatment is to exclude the foodstuffs that upset your Newf's digestion.

Your Newf's diet plays a large role in his overall health and condition, including coat and behavior.

A male dog flea, *Ctenocephalides canis.*

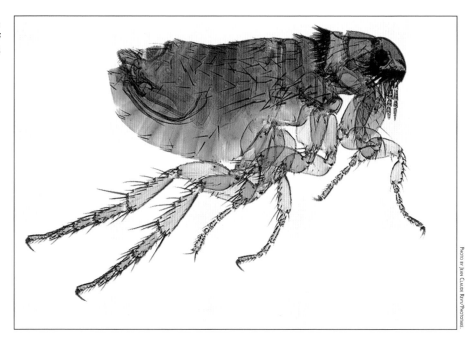

Photo by Jean Claude Revy/Phototake

EXTERNAL PARASITES

FLEAS

Of all the problems to which dogs are prone, none is more well known and frustrating than fleas. Flea infestation is relatively simple to cure but difficult to prevent. Parasites that are harbored inside the body are a bit more difficult to eradicate but they are easier to control.

To control flea infestation, you have to understand the flea's life cycle. Fleas are often thought of as a summertime problem, but centrally heated homes have changed the patterns and fleas can be found at any time of the year. The most effective method of flea control is a two-stage approach: one stage to kill the adult fleas, and the other to control the development of pre-adult fleas. Unfortunately, no single active ingredient is effective against all stages of the life cycle.

FLEA KILLER CAUTION— "POISON"

Flea-killers are poisonous. You should not spray these toxic chemicals on areas of a dog's body that he licks, including his genitals and his face. Flea killers taken internally are a better answer, but check with your vet in case internal therapy is not advised for your dog.

LIFE CYCLE STAGES

During its life, a flea will pass through four life stages: egg, larva, pupa or nymph and adult. The adult stage is the most visible and irritating stage of the flea life cycle, and this is why the majority of flea-control products concentrate on this stage. The fact is that adult fleas account for only 1% of the total flea population, and the other 99% exist in pre-adult stages, i.e., eggs, larvae and nymphs. The pre-adult stages are barely visible to the naked eye.

THE LIFE CYCLE OF THE FLEA

Eggs are laid on the dog, usually in quantities of about 20 or 30, several times a day. The adult female flea must have a blood meal before each egg-laying session. When first laid, the eggs will cling to the dog's hair, as the eggs are still moist. However, they will quickly dry out and fall from the dog, especially if the dog moves around or scratches. Many eggs will fall off in the dog's favorite area or an area in which he spends a lot of time, such as his bed.

Once the eggs fall from the dog onto the carpet or furniture, they will hatch into larvae. This takes from one to ten days. Larvae are not particularly mobile and will usually travel only a few inches from where they hatch. However, they do have a tendency to move away from bright light and heavy

EN GARDE: CATCHING FLEAS OFF GUARD!
Consider the following ways to arm yourself against fleas:
- Add a small amount of pennyroyal or eucalyptus oil to your dog's bath. These natural remedies repel fleas.
- Supplement your dog's food with fresh garlic (minced or grated) and a hearty amount of brewer's yeast, both of which ward off fleas.
- Use a flea comb on your dog daily. Submerge fleas in a cup of bleach to kill them quickly.
- Confine the dog to only a few rooms to limit the spread of fleas in the home.
- Vacuum daily...and get all of the crevices! Dispose of the bag every few days until the problem is under control.
- Wash your dog's bedding daily. Cover cushions where your dog sleeps with towels, and wash the towels often.

traffic—under furniture and behind doors are common places to find high quantities of flea larvae.

The flea larvae feed on dead organic matter, including adult flea feces, until they are ready to change into adult fleas. Fleas will usually remain as larvae for around seven days. After this period, the larvae will pupate into protective pupae. While inside the pupae, the larvae will undergo

Fleas have been measured as being able to jump 300,000 times and can jump over 150 times their length in any direction, including straight up.

metamorphosis and change into adult fleas. This can take as little time as a few days, but the adult fleas can remain inside the pupae waiting to hatch for up to two years. The pupae are signaled to hatch by certain stimuli, such as physical pressure—the pupae's being stepped on, heat from an animal's lying on the pupae or increased carbon-dioxide levels and vibrations—indicating that a suitable host is available.

Once hatched, the adult flea must feed within a few days. Once the adult flea finds a host, it will not leave voluntarily. It only becomes dislodged by grooming or the host animal's scratching.

PHOTO BY DWIGHT R. KUHN

The adult flea will remain on the host for the duration of its life unless forcibly removed.

TREATING THE ENVIRONMENT AND THE DOG

Treating fleas should be a two-pronged attack. First, the environment needs to be treated; this includes carpets and furniture, especially the dog's bedding and areas underneath furniture. The environment should be treated with a household spray containing an Insect Growth Regulator (IGR) and an insecticide to kill the adult fleas. Most IGRs are effective against eggs and larvae; they actually mimic the fleas' own hormones and stop the eggs and larvae from developing into adult fleas. There are currently no treatments available to attack the pupa stage of the life cycle, so the adult insecticide is used to kill the newly hatched adult fleas before they find a host. Most IGRs are active for many months, while

A scanning electron micrograph of a dog or cat flea, *Ctenocephalides*, magnified more than 100x. This image has been colorized for effect.

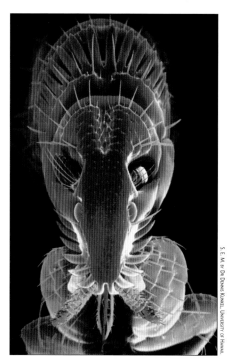

S. E. M. BY DR DENNIS KUNKEL, UNIVERSITY OF HAWAII.

THE LIFE CYCLE OF THE FLEA

Adult

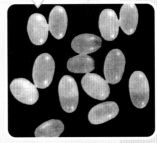

Egg

**Pupa
or
Nymph**

Larva

A LOOK AT FLEAS

Fleas have been around for millions of years and have adapted to changing host animals. They are able to go through a complete life cycle in less than one month or they can extend their lives to almost two years by remaining as pupae or cocoons. They do not need blood or any other food for up to 20 months.

> ## INSECT GROWTH REGULATOR (IGR)
>
> Two types of products should be used when treating fleas—a product to treat the pet and a product to treat the home. Adult fleas represent less than 1% of the flea population. The pre-adult fleas (eggs, larvae and pupae) represent more than 99% of the flea population and are found in the environment; it is in the case of pre-adult fleas that products containing an Insect Growth Regulator (IGR) should be used in the home.
>
> IGRs are a new class of compounds used to prevent the development of insects. They do not kill the insect outright, but instead use the insect's biology against it to stop it from completing its growth. Products that contain methoprene are the world's first and leading IGRs. Used to control fleas and other insects, this type of IGR will stop flea larvae from developing and protect the house for up to seven months.

The American dog tick, *Dermacentor variabilis*, is probably the most common tick found on dogs. Look at the strength in its eight legs! No wonder it's hard to detach them.

adult insecticides are only active for a few days.

When treating with a household spray, it is a good idea to vacuum before applying the product. This stimulates as many pupae as possible to hatch into adult fleas. The vacuum cleaner should also be treated with an insecticide to prevent the eggs and larvae that have been collected in the vacuum bag from hatching.

The second stage of treatment is to apply an adult insecticide to the dog. Traditionally, this would be in the form of a collar or a spray, but more recent innovations include digestible insecticides that poison the fleas when they ingest the dog's blood. Alternatively, there are drops that, when placed on the back of the dog's neck, spread throughout the dog's hair and skin to kill adult fleas.

TICKS

Though not as common as fleas, ticks are found all over the tropical and temperate world. They don't bite, like fleas; they harpoon. They dig their sharp proboscis (nose) into the dog's skin and drink the blood. Their

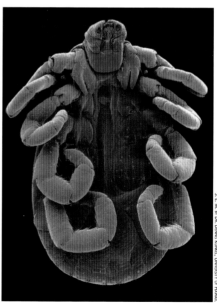

S. E. M. BY DR. DENNIS KUNKEL, UNIVERSITY OF HAWAII.

only food and drink is dog's blood. Dogs can get Lyme disease, Rocky Mountain spotted fever, tick bite paralysis and many other diseases from ticks. They may live where fleas are found and they like to hide in cracks or seams in walls. They are controlled the same way fleas are controlled.

The American dog tick, *Dermacentor variabilis*, may well be the most common dog tick in many geographical areas, especially those areas where the climate is hot and humid. Most dog ticks have life expectancies of a week to six months, depending upon climatic conditions. They can neither jump nor fly, but they can crawl slowly and can range up to 16 feet to reach a sleeping or unsuspecting dog.

MITES

Just as fleas and ticks can be problematic for your dog, mites can also lead to an itchy nuisance. Microscopic in size, mites are related to ticks and generally take up permanent residence on their host animal—in this case, your dog! The term *mange* refers to any infestation caused by one of the mighty mites, of which there are six varieties that concern dog owners.

Demodex mites cause a condition known as demodicosis

DEER-TICK CROSSING

The great outdoors may be fun for your dog, but it also is home to dangerous ticks. Deer ticks carry a bacterium known as *Borrelia burgdorferi* and are most active in the autumn and spring. When infections are caught early, penicillin and tetracycline are effective antibiotics, but, if left untreated, the bacteria may cause neurological, kidney and cardiac problems as well as long-term trouble with walking and painful joints.

S. E. M. BY DR. ANDREW SPIELMAN/PHOTOTAKE.

PHOTO BY DR. DENNIS KUNKEL, UNIVERSITY OF HAWAII.

The head of an American dog tick, *Dermacentor variabilis*, enlarged and colorized for effect.

The mange mite, *Psoroptes bovis*, can infest cattle and other domestic animals.

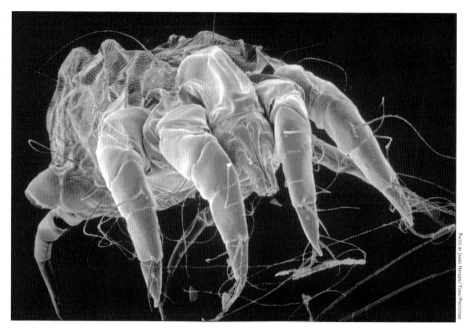

PHOTO BY JAMES HAYDEN/YOAV/PHOTOTAKE

(sometimes called red mange or follicular mange), in which the mites live in the dog's hair follicles and sebaceous glands in larger-than-normal amounts. This type of mange is commonly passed from the dam to her puppies and usually shows up on the puppies' muzzles, though demodicosis is not transferable from one normal dog to another. Most dogs recover from this type of mange without any treatment, though topical therapies are commonly prescribed by the vet.

Human lice look like dog lice; the two are closely related.

PHOTO BY DWIGHT R. KUHN.

The *Cheyletiellosis* mite is the hook-mouthed culprit associated with "walking dandruff," a condition that affects dogs as well as cats and rabbits. This mite lives on the surface of the animal's skin and is readily transferable through direct or indirect contact with an affected animal. The dandruff is present in the form of scaly skin, which may or may not be itchy. If not treated, this mange can affect a whole kennel of dogs and can be spread to humans as well.

The *Sarcoptes* mite causes intense itching on the dog in the form of a condition known as scabies or sarcoptic mange. The cycle of the *Sarcoptes* mite lasts about three weeks, and the mites live in the top layer of the dog's skin (epidermis), preferably in areas with little hair. Scabies is highly contagious and can be passed to humans. Sometimes an allergic reaction to the mite worsens the severe itching associated with sarcoptic mange.

Ear mites, *Otodectes cynotis,* lead to otodectic mange, which most commonly affects the outer ear canal of the dog, though other areas can be affected as well. Dogs with ear-mite infestation commonly scratch at their ears, causing further irritation, and shake their heads. Dark brown droppings in the outer ear confirm the diagnosis. Your vet can prescribe a treatment to flush out the ears and kill any eggs in the ears. A complete month of treatment is necessary to cure the mange.

Two other mites, less common in dogs, include *Dermanyssus gallinae* (the poultry or red mite) and *Eutrombicula alfreddugesi* (the North American mite associated with trombiculidiasis or chigger infestation). The poultry mite frequently lives on chickens, but can transfer to dogs who spend time near farm animals. Chigger infestation affects dogs in the

> **NOT A DROP TO DRINK**
> Never allow your dog to swim in polluted water or public areas where water quality can be suspect. Even perfectly clear water can harbor parasites, many of which can cause serious to fatal illnesses in canines. Areas inhabited by water-fowl and other wildlife are especially dangerous.

central US who have exposure to woodlands. The types of mange caused by both of these mites are treatable by veterinarians.

INTERNAL PARASITES

Most animals—fishes, birds and mammals, including dogs and humans—have worms and other parasites that live inside their bodies. According to Dr. Herbert R. Axelrod, the fish pathologist, there are two kinds of parasites: dumb and smart. The smart parasites live in peaceful cooperation with their hosts (symbiosis), while the dumb parasites kill their hosts. Most worm infections are relatively easy to control. If they are not controlled, they weaken the host dog to the point that other medical problems occur, but they do not kill the host as dumb parasites would.

A brown dog tick, *Rhipicephalus sanguineus*, is an uncommon but annoying tick found on dogs.

> **DO NOT MIX**
> Never mix parasite-control products without first consulting your vet. Some products can become toxic when combined with others and can cause fatal consequences.

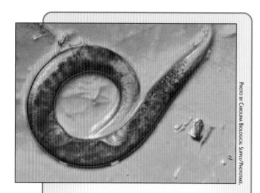

The roundworm *Rhabditis* can infect both dogs and humans.

The roundworm, *Ascaris lumbricoides*.

PHOTO BY CAROLINA BIOLOGICAL SUPPLY/PHOTOTAKE.

ROUNDWORMS

Average-size dogs can pass 1,360,000 roundworm eggs every day. For example, if there were only 1 million dogs in the world, the world would be saturated with thousands of tons of dog feces. These feces would contain around 15,000,000,000 roundworm eggs.

Up to 31% of home yards and children's sand boxes in the US contain roundworm eggs.

Flushing dog's feces down the toilet is not a safe practice because the usual sewage treatments do not destroy roundworm eggs.

Infected puppies start shedding roundworm eggs at three weeks of age. They can be infected by their mother's milk.

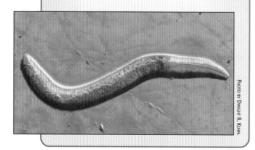

PHOTO BY DWIGHT R. KUHN.

ROUNDWORMS

The roundworms that infect dogs are known scientifically as *Toxocara canis*. They live in the dog's intestines and shed eggs continually. It has been estimated that a dog produces about 6 or more ounces of feces every day. Each ounce of feces averages hundreds of thousands of roundworm eggs. There are no known areas in which dogs roam that do not contain roundworm eggs. The greatest danger of roundworms is that they infect people, too! It is wise to have your dog tested regularly for roundworms.

In young puppies, roundworms cause bloated bellies, diarrhea, coughing and vomiting, and are transmitted from the dam (through blood or milk). Affected puppies will not appear as animated as normal puppies. The worms appear spaghetti-like, measuring as long as 6 inches. Adult dogs can acquire roundworms through coprophagia (eating contaminated feces) or by killing rodents that carry roundworms.

Roundworm infection can kill puppies and cause severe problems in adults, as the hatched larvae travel to the lungs and trachea through the bloodstream. Cleanliness is the best preventative for roundworms. Always pick up after your dog and dispose of feces in appropriate receptacles.

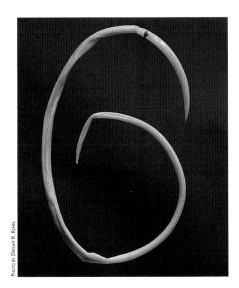

HOOKWORMS

In the United States, dog owners have to be concerned about four different species of hookworm, the most common and most serious of which is *Ancylostoma caninum,* which prefers warm climates. The others are *Ancylostoma braziliense, Ancylostoma tubaeforme* and *Uncinaria stenocephala,* the latter of which is a concern to dogs living in the northern US and Canada, as this species prefers cold climates. Hookworms are dangerous to humans as well as to dogs and cats, and can be the cause of severe anemia due to iron deficiency. The worm uses its teeth to attach itself to the dog's intestines and changes the site of its attachment about six times per day. Each time the worm repositions itself, the dog loses blood and can become anemic. *Ancylostoma caninum* is the most likely of the four species to cause anemia in the dog.

Symptoms of hookworm infection include dark stools, weight loss, general weakness, pale coloration and anemia, as well as possible skin problems. Fortunately, hookworms are easily purged from the affected dog with a number of medications that have proven effective. Discuss these with your veterinarian. Most heartworm preventatives include a hookworm insecticide as well.

Owners also must be aware that hookworms can infect humans, who can acquire the larvae through exposure to contaminated feces. Since the worms cannot complete their life cycle on a human, the worms simply infest the skin and cause irritation. This condition is known as cutaneous larva migrans syndrome. As a preventative, use disposable gloves or a "poop-scoop" to pick up your dog's droppings and prevent your dog (or neighborhood cats) from defecating in children's play areas.

The hookworm, *Ancylostoma caninum.*

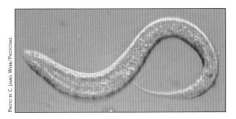

The infective stage of the hookworm larva.

TAPEWORMS

Humans, rats, squirrels, foxes, coyotes, wolves and domestic dogs are all susceptible to tapeworm infection. Except in humans, tapeworms are usually not a fatal infection. Infected individuals can harbor 1000 parasitic worms.

Tapeworms, like some other types of worm, are hermaphroditic, meaning male and female in the same worm.

If dogs eat infected rats or mice, or anything else infected with tapeworm, they get the tapeworm disease. One month after attaching to a dog's intestine, the worm starts shedding eggs. These eggs are infective immediately. Infective eggs can live for a few months without a host animal.

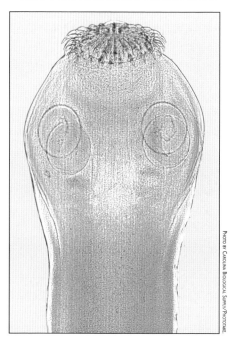

The head and rostellum (the round prominence on the scolex) of a tapeworm, which infects dogs and humans.

PHOTO BY CAROLINA BIOLOGICAL SUPPLY/PHOTOTAKE.

TAPEWORMS

There are many species of tapeworm, all of which are carried by fleas! The most common tapeworm affecting dogs is known as *Dipylidium caninum*. The dog eats the flea and starts the tapeworm cycle. Humans can also be infected with tapeworms—so don't eat fleas! Fleas are so small that your dog could pass them onto your hands, your plate or your food and thus make it possible for you to ingest a flea that is carrying tapeworm eggs.

While tapeworm infection is not life-threatening in dogs (smart parasite!), it can be the cause of a very serious liver disease for humans. About 50% of the humans infected with *Echinococcus multilocularis*, a type of tapeworm that causes alveolar hydatid, perish.

WHIPWORMS

In North America, whipworms are counted among the most common parasitic worms in dogs. The whipworm's scientific name is *Trichuris vulpis*. These worms attach themselves in the lower parts of the intestine, where they feed. Affected dogs may only experience upset tummies, colic and diarrhea. These worms, however, can live for months or years in the dog, beginning their larval stage in the small intestine, spending their adult stage in the large intestine and finally passing infective eggs through the dog's feces. The only way to detect whipworms is through a fecal examination, though this is not always foolproof. Treatment for whipworms is tricky, due to the worms' unusual life-cycle pattern, and very often dogs are reinfected due to exposure to infective eggs on the ground. The whipworm eggs can survive in the environment for as long as five years; thus, cleaning up droppings in your own backyard as well as in public places is absolutely essential for sanitation purposes and the health of your dog and others.

THREADWORMS

Though less common than round-worms, hookworms and those previously mentioned, thread-worms concern dog owners in the southwestern US and Gulf Coast area, where the climate is hot and humid. Living in the small intestine of the dog, this worm measures a mere 2 millimeters and is round in shape. Like that of the whipworm, the threadworm's life cycle is very complex and the eggs and larvae are passed through the feces. A deadly disease in humans, *Strongyloides* readily infects people, and the handling of feces is the most common means of transmission. Threadworms are most often seen in young puppies; bloody diarrhea and pneumonia are symptoms. Sick puppies must be isolated and treated immediately; vets recommend a follow-up treatment one month later.

HEARTWORM PREVENTATIVES

There are many heartworm preventatives on the market, many of which are sold at your veterinarian's office. These products can be given daily or monthly, depending on the manufacturer's instructions. All of these preventatives contain chemical insecticides directed at killing heartworms, which leads to some controversy among dog owners. In effect, heartworm preventatives are necessary evils, though you should determine how necessary based on your pet's lifestyle. There is no doubt that heartworm is a dreadful disease that threatens the lives of dogs. However, the likelihood of your dog's being bitten by an infected mosquito is slim in most places, and a mosquito-repellent (or an herbal remedy such as Wormwood or Black Walnut) is much safer for your dog and will not compromise his immune system (the way heartworm preventatives will). Should you decide to use the traditional preventative "medications," you can consider giving the pill every other or third month. Since the toxins in the pill will kill the heartworms at all stages of development, the pill would be effective in killing larvae, nymphs or adults and it takes four months for the larvae to reach the adult stage. Thus, there is no rationale to poisoning the dog's system on a monthly basis. Lastly, do not give the pill during the winter months since there are no mosquitoes around to pass on their infection, unless you live in a tropical environment.

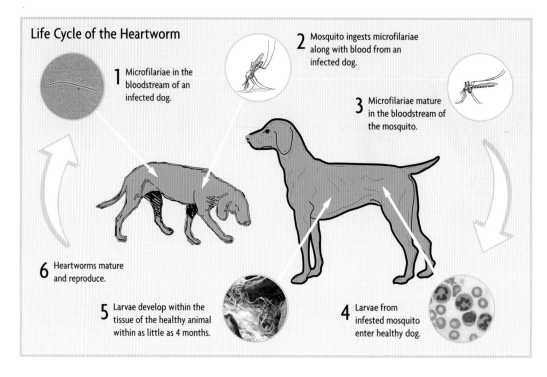

Life Cycle of the Heartworm

1 Microfilariae in the bloodstream of an infected dog.

2 Mosquito ingests microfilariae along with blood from an infected dog.

3 Microfilariae mature in the bloodstream of the mosquito.

4 Larvae from infested mosquito enter healthy dog.

5 Larvae develop within the tissue of the healthy animal within as little as 4 months.

6 Heartworms mature and reproduce.

HEARTWORMS

Heartworms are thin, extended worms up to 12 inches long, which live in a dog's heart and the major blood vessels surrounding it. Dogs may have up to 200 worms. Symptoms may be loss of energy, loss of appetite, coughing, the development of a pot belly and anemia.

Heartworms are transmitted by mosquitoes. The mosquito drinks the blood of an infected dog and takes in larvae with the blood. The larvae, called microfilariae, develop within the body of the mosquito and are passed on to the next dog bitten after the larvae mature. It takes two to three weeks for the larvae to develop to the infective stage within the body of the mosquito. Dogs are usually treated at about six weeks of age and maintained on a prophylactic dose given monthly.

Blood testing for heartworms is not necessarily indicative of how seriously your dog is infected. Although this is a dangerous disease, it is not easy for a dog to be infected. Discuss the various preventatives with your vet, as there are many different types now available. Together you can decide on a safe course of prevention for your dog.

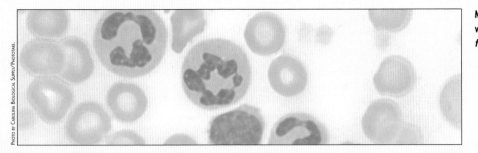

Magnified heart-
worm larvae, *Diro-
filaria immitis.*

PHOTO BY CAROLINA BIOLOGICAL SUPPLY/PHOTOTAKE.

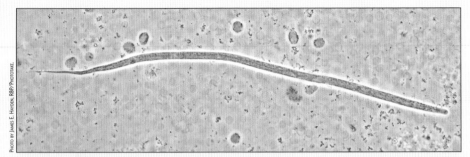

Heartworm, *Diro-
filaria immitis.*

PHOTO BY JAMES E. HAYDEN, RBP/PHOTOTAKE.

The heart
of a dog infected
with canine heart-
worm, *Dirofilaria
immitis.*

PHOTO BY JAMES E. HAYDEN, RBP/PHOTOTAKE.

HOMEOPATHY:
an alternative to conventional medicine

"Less is Most"

Using this principle, the strength of a homeopathic remedy is measured by the number of serial dilutions that were undertaken to create it. The greater the number of serial dilutions, the greater the strength of the homeopathic remedy. The potency of a remedy that has been made by making a dilution of 1 part in 100 parts (or 1/100) is 1c or 1cH. If this remedy is subjected to a series of further dilutions, each one being 1/100, a more dilute and stronger remedy is produced. If the remedy is diluted in this way six times, it is called 6c or 6cH. A dilution of 6c is 1 part in 1,000,000,000,000. In general, higher potencies in more frequent doses are better for acute symptoms and lower potencies in more infrequent doses are more useful for chronic, long-standing problems.

CURING OUR DOGS NATURALLY

Holistic medicine means treating the whole animal as a unique, perfect, living being. Generally, holistic treatments do not suppress the symptoms that the body naturally produces, as do most medications prescribed by conventional doctors and vets. Holistic methods seek to cure disease by regaining balance and harmony in the patient's environment. Some of these methods include use of nutritional therapy, herbs, flower essences, aromatherapy, acupuncture, massage, chiropractic and, of course, the most popular holistic approach, homeopathy.

Homeopathy is a theory or system of treating illness with small doses of substances which, if administered in larger quantities, would produce the symptoms that the patient already has. This approach is often described as "like cures like." Although modern veterinary medicine is geared toward the "quick fix," homeopathy relies on the belief that, given the time, the body is able to heal itself and return to its natural, healthy state.

Choosing a remedy to cure a problem in our dogs is the difficult part of homeopathy. Consult with your vet for a professional diagnosis of your dog's symptoms. Often these symptoms require immediate conventional care. If your vet is willing and knowledgeable, you may attempt a homeopathic remedy. Be aware that cortisone prevents homeopathic remedies from working. There are hundreds of possibilities and combinations to cure many problems in dogs, from basic physical problems such as excessive shedding, fleas or other parasites, unattractive doggy odor, bad breath, upset tummy, obesity, dry, oily or dull coat, diarrhea, ear problems and eye discharge (including tears and dry or mucousy matter), to behavioral abnormalities such as fear of loud noises, habitual licking, poor appetite, excessive barking and various phobias. From alumina to zincum metallicum, the remedies span the planet and the imagination…from flowers and weeds to chemicals, insect droppings, diesel smoke and volcanic ash.

Using "Like to Treat Like"

Unlike conventional medicines that suppress symptoms, homeopathic remedies treat illnesses with small doses of substances that, if administered in larger quantities, would produce the symptoms that the patient already has. While the same homeopathic remedy can be used to treat different symptoms in different dogs, here are some interesting remedies and their uses.

Apis Mellifica
(made from honey bee venom) can be used for allergies or to reduce swelling that occurs in acutely infected kidneys.

Diesel Smoke
can be used to help control travel sickness.

Calcarea Fluorica
(made from calcium fluoride, which helps harden bone structure) can be useful in treating hard lumps in tissues.

Natrum Muriaticum
(made from common salt, sodium chloride) is useful in treating thin, thirsty dogs.

Nitricum Acidum
(made from nitric acid) is used for symptoms you would expect to see from contact with acids, such as lesions, especially where the skin joins the linings of body orifices or openings such as the lips and nostrils.

Symphytum
(made from the herb Knitbone, *Symphytum officianale*) is used to encourage bones to heal.

Urtica Urens
(made from the common stinging nettle) is used in treating painful, irritating rashes.

First Aid at a Glance

Burns
Place the affected area under cool water; use ice if only a small area is burnt.

Bee stings/Insect bites
Apply ice to relieve swelling; antihistamine dosed properly.

Animal bites
Clean any bleeding area; apply pressure until bleeding subsides; go to the vet.

Spider bites
Use cold compress and a pressurized pack to inhibit venom's spreading.

Antifreeze poisoning
Induce vomiting with hydrogen peroxide. Seek *immediate* veterinary help!

Fish hooks
Removal best handled by vet; hook must be cut in order to remove.

Snake bites
Pack ice around bite; contact vet quickly; identify snake for proper antivenin.

Car accident
Move dog from roadway with blanket; seek veterinary aid.

Shock
Calm the dog; keep him warm; seek immediate veterinary help.

Nosebleed
Apply cold compress to the nose; apply pressure to any visible abrasion.

Bleeding
Apply pressure above the area; treat wound by applying a cotton pack.

Heat stroke
Submerge dog in cold bath; cool down with fresh air and water; go to the vet.

Frostbite/Hypothermia
Warm the dog with a warm bath, electric blankets or hot water bottles.

Abrasions
Clean the wound and wash out thoroughly with fresh water; apply antiseptic.

 Remember: an injured dog may attempt to bite a helping hand from fear and confusion. Always muzzle the dog before trying to offer assistance.

NEWFOUNDLAND

The term *old* is a qualitative term. For dogs, as well as their masters, old is relative. Certainly we can all distinguish between a puppy Newfoundland and an adult Newfoundland—there are the obvious physical traits, such as size, appearance and facial expressions, and personality traits as well. Puppies and young dogs like to play with children. Children's natural exuberance is a good match for the seemingly endless energy of young dogs. They like to run, jump, chase and retrieve. When dogs grow older and cease their interaction with children, they are often thought of as being too old to play with the kids.

On the other hand, if a Newfoundland is only exposed to people with quieter lifestyles, his life will normally be less active and the decrease in his activity level as he ages will not be as obvious.

If people live to be 100 years old, dogs live to be 20 years old. While this may sound like a convenient rule of thumb, it is *very* inaccurate. When trying to compare dog years to human years, you cannot make a generalization about all dogs. You can

make the generalization that eight to ten years is the average lifespan for a Newfoundland, which is not terribly long compared to many smaller breeds and reminds us how precious our time with our beloved Newfs truly is.

Dogs generally are considered mature at three years of age (or earlier), but can reproduce even earlier. So it is more viable to say that the first three years of a dog's life are like seven times that of comparable humans. That means a 3-year-old dog is like a 21-year-old human. As the curve of comparison shows, however, there

The Newf is still an alert companion in his senior years.

is no hard and fast rule for comparing dog and human ages. The comparison is made even more difficult, for not all humans age at the same rate.

WHAT TO LOOK FOR IN SENIORS

Most veterinarians and behaviorists use the six- or seven-year mark as the time to consider a Newf a "senior." The term "senior" does not imply that the dog is geriatric and has begun to fail in mind and body. Aging is essentially a slowing process. Humans readily admit that they feel a difference in their activity level from age 20 to 30, and then from 30 to 40, etc. By treating the six- or seven-year-old dog as a senior, owners are able to implement certain therapeutic and preventative medical strategies with the help of their vets.

HORMONAL PROBLEMS

Although graying is normal and expected in older dogs, a flaky coat or loss of hair is not. Such coat problems may point to a hormonal problem. Hypothyroidism, in which the thyroid gland fails to produce the normal amount of hormones, is one such problem. Your veterinarian can treat hypothyroidism with an oral supplement. The condition is more common in certain breeds, so discuss its likelihood in your dog with your breeder and vet.

A senior-care program should include at least two veterinary visits per year and screening sessions to determine the dog's health status, as well as nutritional counseling. Veterinarians determine the senior dog's health status through a blood smear for a complete blood count, serum chemistry profile with electrolytes, urinalysis, blood pressure check, electrocardiogram, ocular tonometry (pressure on the eyeball) and dental prophylaxis.

Such an extensive program for senior dogs is well advised before owners start to see the obvious physical signs of aging, such as slower and inhibited movement, graying, increased sleep/nap periods and disinterest in play and other activity. This preventative program promises a longer, healthier life for the aging dog. Among the physical problems common in aging dogs are the loss of sight and hearing, arthritis, kidney and liver failure, diabetes mellitus, heart disease and Cushing's disease (a hormonal disease).

In addition to the physical manifestations discussed, there are some behavioral changes and problems related to aging dogs. Dogs suffering from hearing or vision loss, dental discomfort or arthritis can become aggressive. Likewise, the near-deaf and/or blind dog may be startled more easily and react in an unexpectedly aggressive manner. Seniors suffering from senility can become more impatient and irritable. Housesoiling accidents are associated with loss of mobility, kidney problems and loss of sphincter control as well as plaque accumulation, physiological brain changes and reactions to medications. Older dogs, just like young puppies, can suffer from separation anxiety, which can lead to excessive barking, whining, housesoiling and destructive behavior. Seniors may become fearful of everyday sounds, such as vacuum cleaners, heaters, thun-

der and passing traffic. Some dogs have difficulty sleeping, due to discomfort, the need for frequent toilet visits and the like.

Owners should avoid spoiling the older dog with too many treats. Obesity is a common problem in older dogs and subtracts years from their lives. Keep the senior dog as trim as possible since excess weight puts additional stress on the body's vital organs. Some breeders recommend supplementing the diet with foods high in fiber and lower in calories. Adding fresh vegetables and marrow broth to

A proud senior Newfie with his graying muzzle. Older Newfs naturally take life easier and welcome periodic rests throughout the day.

the senior's diet makes a tasty, low-calorie, low-fat supplement. Vets also offer specialty diets for senior dogs that are worth exploring.

Your dog, as he nears his twilight years, needs his owner's patience and good care more than ever. Never punish an older dog for an accident or abnormal behavior. For all the years of love, protection and companionship that your dog has provided, he deserves special attention and courtesies. The older dog may need to relieve himself at 3 a.m. because he can no longer "hold it" for eight hours. Older dogs may not be able to remain crated for more than two or three hours. It may be time to give up a sofa to your old friend. Although he may not seem as enthusiastic about your attention and petting, he does appreciate the considerations you offer as he gets older.

Your Newfoundland does not understand why his world is slowing down. Owners must make their dogs' transition into their golden years as pleasant and rewarding as possible.

WHAT TO DO WHEN THE TIME COMES

You are never fully prepared to make a rational decision about putting your dog to sleep. It is very obvious that you love your Newfoundland or you would not be reading this book. Putting a

---

AGING ADDITIVES

A healthy diet is important for dogs of all ages, but older dogs may benefit from the addition of supplements like antioxidants, which fight the aging process, and vitamin B, which aids the kidneys. Check with your vet before adding these or any supplements to your pet's diet.

---

loved dog to sleep is extremely difficult. It is a decision that must be made with your veterinarian. You are usually forced to make the decision when your dog experiences one or more life-threatening symptoms, requiring you to seek medical (veterinary) help.

If the prognosis of the malady indicates the end is near and your beloved pet will only suffer more and experience no enjoyment for the balance of his life, then euthanasia is the right choice.

WHAT IS EUTHANASIA?

Euthanasia derives from the Greek, meaning *good death*. In other words, it means the planned, painless killing of a dog suffering from a painful, incurable condition, or who is so aged that he cannot walk, see, eat or control his excretory functions.

Euthanasia is usually accomplished by injection with an overdose of an anesthesia or barbiturate. Aside from the prick of the needle, the experience is usually painless.

MAKING THE DECISION

The decision to euthanize your dog is never easy. The days during which the dog becomes ill and the end occurs can be unusually stressful for you. If this is your first experience with the death of a loved one, you may need the comfort dictated by your religious beliefs. If you are the head of the family and have children, you should have involved them in the decision of putting your Newfoundland to sleep. Usually your dog can be maintained on drugs for a few days in order to give you ample time to make a decision. During this time, talking with members of your family, clergy members or even people who have lived through this same experience can ease the burden of your inevitable decision.

THE FINAL RESTING PLACE

Dogs can have some of the same privileges as humans. The remains of your beloved dog can be buried in a pet cemetery, which is generally expensive. If your dog has died at home, he can be buried in your yard in a place suitably marked with a special stone or newly planted tree or bush. Alternatively, dogs can be cremated individually and the ashes returned to you. A less expensive option is mass crema-

tion, although, of course, the ashes of individual dogs cannot then be returned. Vets can usually help you locate a pet cemetery or help arrange the cremation on your behalf. The cost of these options should always be discussed frankly and openly with your veterinarian.

GETTING ANOTHER DOG?

The grief of losing your beloved dog will be as lasting as the grief of losing a human friend or relative. In most cases, if your dog died of old age (if there is such a thing), he had slowed down considerably. Do you now want a new Newfoundland puppy? Or are you better off finding a more mature Newfoundland, say two to three years of age, which will usually be house-trained and will have an already developed personality. In this case, you can find out if you like each other after a few hours of being together.

The decision is, of course, your own. Do you want another Newfoundland or perhaps a different breed so as to avoid comparison with your beloved friend? Most people usually stay with the same breed because they know (and love) the characteristics of that breed. Then, too, they often know people who have the same breed and perhaps they are lucky enough that a breeder they know and respect expects a litter soon. What could be better?

INDEX

Page numbers in **boldface** indicate illustrations.

Activities 107-117
Adult
—diet 65
—health 126
—training 85
Affection 21
Age 91
Aggression 58
—fear 103
Agility trials 113
Aging 152
Air travel 80
Alaska 17
Aleutian Islands 17
All-breed show 108-109
Allergy
—airborne 130
—food 130
—parasite bite 128
—vaccine 126
American dog tick **138-139**
American Kennel Club 17, 34, 108
—groups 110
—standard 27
Anal sacs 128
Ancylostoma braziliense 143
Ancylostoma caninum **143**
Ancylostoma tubaeforme 143
Ascaris lumbricoides **142**
Attention 21, 97
Auto-immune skin conditions 129
Axelrod, Dr. Herbert R. 141
Backpacking 116-117
Baron 17
Bathing 72, 75
Bear Dogs 9
Bedding 45, 61, 90
Beothuk Indians 9
Best in Show 109
Best of Breed 109
Best of Opposite Sex 109
Best of Winners 109
Bland, Mr. G. 13
Bloat 24, 50, 68, 132-133
Boarding 81
Boatswain 18
Bonaparte, Napoleon 10
Bones 47
Booster shots 123, 126
Boredom 21
Borrelia burgdorferi 139
Bowls 48
Brave Michael **12**
Breed club 34, 108
Breeder 33-34, 36, 55
Brown dog tick **141**
Brushing 71
Burial 155
Byron, Lord 18
Cabin Boy 17
Canada 17, 113
Cancer 127

Canine cough 123-125
Canine development schedule 91
Canine Good Citizen® program 109
Car travel 79
Carting 116-117
Cartwright, George 15
Cat 96
Cataracts 129
Champion 109
Champion Tracker 116
Chesapeake Bay Retriever 15-16
Chewing 46, 52, 92
Cheyletiellosis 140
Children 9, 21, 58
Chocolate 60
Class dogs 108
Classes at shows 108, 112
Climbing 53
Coat 21, 22, 69-76
Collar 48, 96
Color 22
Colostrum 64
Come 101
Commands 98-106
Commitment of ownership 37
Conformation showing 108
Conjunctivitis 129
Consistency 58-59, 104
Control 89
Copus, Mr. E. Heden 12
Corneal damage 129
Cornwall and York, Duke and Duchess of 17
Coronavirus 124-125
Crate 43-44, 61, 80
—training 44, 87-95
Cremation 155
Crying 56, 60
Ctenocephalides **136**
Ctenocephalides canis **134**
Currier and Ives 13
Cushing's disease 130
Cutaneous larva migrans syndrome 143
Cystinuria 23
Daventry Coastguard 11
Deer tick **139**
Delivery work 11
Demodex 139
Dental health 121, 124, 126
Dermacentor variabilis **138-139**
Dermanyssus gallinae 141
Destructive behavior 92, 153
Diet 21, 55, 132, 62-66
—adult 65
—puppy 63
—senior 65, 153, 155
Digging 53
Dipylidium caninum 144
Dirofilaria immitis **147**
Discipline 95
Distemper 16, 123-125
Dominance 58
Double coat 12

Down 99
Down/stay 101
Draft tests 116
Drooling 21
Dry eye 129
Ear
—cleaning 76
—mite infestation 76, 141
Echinococcus multilocularis 144
England 17, 19
Ericsson, Leif 9
Euthanasia 154
Eutrombicula alfreddugesi 141
Exercise 21, 68, 80
External parasites 134-141
Eye disease 129
Family dog 9
Fear period 58
Feeding 21, 62-66, 132
Fence 53
First aid 150
Flea **134**, 135, **136**, **137**, 138
Food 55, 62, 62-66
—allergies 130-133
—bowls 50
—intolerance 133
—rewards 97, 100, 106
—types of 62-63
Gastric dilatation 24, 50, 68, 132-133
Gentle giant 9
Glaucoma 129
Grooming 21, 69-79
—equipment 72
Group show 108-109
Growth period 65
"He is Saved" 13
Health
—adult 126
—dental 121
—puppy 123
Heart condition 23
Heartworm 124, 145, **146-147**
Heel 105
Hepatitis 123-125
Hereditary skin disorders 127
Hip dysplasia **25**, 124
Holistic medicine 148-149
Home preparation for pup 40
Hookworm **143**
Hormonal problems 152
Hormones 85, 87
House-training 87-95
Housing 89
Hypothyroidism 152
Identification 82-83
Insect Growth Regulator 136, 138
Internal parasites 141-147
Labrador Retriever 15
Landseer variety **14-15**, 26
Landseer, Sir Edwin 13-15
Lead 47, 96
Leptospirosis 124-125

Lewis and Clark expedition 11
Lice **140**
Lifeguard dog 9
Lifespan 22, 151
Litter size 36
Lupus 129
MacCormack, Sir William 15
Macpherson, Hon. Harold, L.L.D. 17
Mange 139-141
—mite **140**
Mastiff 9
Mats 71
Maturity 22, 65, 151
McCann, Mrs. F. 16
Mermaid **13**
Microchip 83
Milk 64, 133
Milk Boy **10**
Mites 139, **140**, 141
Mulch 60
Nail clipping 78
Nana 16
National Gallery of British Art 14
Negative reinforcement 95
Neptune 17
Netherwood Queen **16**
Neutering 124
Newfoundland Club of America 17, 34, 108, 112
Newfoundland Club of Denmark 113
Newfoundland, King of 11
Newstead Abbey 19
Nipping 60
North America 9, 10, 17
North American Newfoundland Club 17
Northern Newfoundland Club 112
Nutrition 65
Obedience classes 84, 87, 107
Obedience competition 107
Obesity 62, 64, 66, 153
Onions 60
Origin of breed 9
Orthopedic Foundation for Animals 22
Otodectes cynotis 141
Outer coat 12
Ownership 38
Parainfluenza 123-124
Parasite
—bite 128
—external 134-141
—internal 141-147
Parent club 108
Parvovirus 123-125
Patent ductus arteriosus 23
Personality 9, 21-22
Peter Pan 16
Plants 51, 131
Poisons 51-53, 60, 131
Pollen allergies 130
Portuguese Water Dog 9
Positive reinforcement 87, 95
Postal work 11

Praise 87, 97, 99, 107
Preventative medicine 121
Psoroptes bovis **140**
Pulmonic stenosis 23
Punishment 95-96
Puppy
—appearance 32
—family introduction 54
—financial responsibility 48
—first night home 55
—first trip to the vet 53
—food 63
—health 123
—ownership 37
—preparing home for 40
—problems 57, 59, 61
—selection 34
—temperament 38, 43
—training 58-59, 85
Puppy-proofing 51, 53
Pyrenean Sheepdog 9
Rabies 124-125
Rescue dogs 10-15, 109
Reserve Winners Bitch 109
Reserve Winners Dog 108
Rest, V. D. 18
Retrieving dogs 9
Rewards 55, 95, 97, 100, 107
Rhabditis **142**
Rhipicephalus sanguineus **141**
Roundworm **142**
Safety 51-52, 80, 89, 92
St. Bernard 16
St. Johns 11
Sarcoptes **140**
"Saved" 13
Scabies **140**
Seasonal Affected Disorder 71
Senior
—care of 152
—diet 65, 153, 155
Separation anxiety 61, 153
Shedding 21, 71, 75
Showing 108
Siki 17
Sit 98
Sit/stay 100
Size 9
Skin problems 126-130
Smiling 40
Socialization 57
Spaying 124
Specials 109
Specialty show 108
Standard 26, 109
—AKC 27
Stay 100
Strongyloides 145
Sub-valvular aortic stenosis 23
Success Method 94
Supplements 62
Swansea Jack 10

Swimming ability 10, 12, 110
Tapeworm **144**
Tattoo 83
Tedder, Paul & Christine 112
Temperament 9, 21-22
Thebromine 60
Thorndike's Theory of Learning 95
Thorndike, Dr. Edward 95
Threadworms 145
Tibetan Mastiff 9
Tick **138-139, 141**
Titanic 11
Toxic plants 51, 131
Toxins 51-53, 60
Toxocara canis **142**
Toys 45-47, 61, 90
Tracheobronchitis 123
Tracking 116
Training
—adult 85
—commands 98-106
—consistency 58-59, 104
—crate 87-95
—equipment 96
—for water activities 110
—puppy 58-59, 85
Traveling 79-82
Treats 55, 60, 96, 99, 107
Trichuris vulpis 144
Tricuspid valvular dysplasia 23
Types of shows 108
Uncinaria stenocephala 143
Undercoat 12
United States 17
Urinary-tract disease 24, 123
Vacations 81
Vaccinations 58, 123-124
—allergies 126
Versatile Surface Tracking 116
Veterinarian 53, 119, 126, 141
Veterinary dermatologist 127
Veterinary specialties 119
Vikings 9
Viruses 123
Water 68, 90
—activities 109-112
—bowls 50
—dogs 12-15
Weaning 64
Westerland kennel 17
Whining 56, 60
Whipworms 144
Winners Bitch 108
Winners Dog 108
Wolves 9
Working dogs 10-12, 109
Working Rescue Dog 113
World War I 17
World War II 13, 17
Worm control 124
Yard 53

My Newfoundland

PUT YOUR PUPPY'S FIRST PICTURE HERE

Dog's Name _____

Date _____ Photographer _____